Dorothea Ruggles-Brise

The Edinburgh musical miscellany;

Or modern songster: a collection of the most approved Scotch, English, and Irish

songs, set to music

Dorothea Ruggles-Brise

The Edinburgh musical miscellany;
Or modern songster: a collection of the most approved Scotch, English, and Irish songs, set to music

ISBN/EAN: 9783337728632

Printed in Europe, USA, Canada, Australia, Japan

Cover: Foto ©ninafisch / pixelio.de

More available books at **www.hansebooks.com**

THE

EDINBURGH

MUSICAL MISCELLANY;

OR

MODERN SONGSTER:

A

COLLECTION

OF THE MOST APPROVED

SCOTCH, ENGLISH, AND IRISH

SONGS,

SET TO MUSIC.

EDINBURGH,
Printed for John Elder, T. Brown, and C. Elliot,
Edinburgh; and W. Coke, *Leith*.

M,DCC,XCIII.

TO THE PUBLIC.

THE favourable reception which the firſt volume of the Edinburgh Muſical Miſcellany met with, has induced the Editors to bring forward a ſecond Volume, conducted upon a ſimilar plan, ſelected, they hope, with equal judgment and taſte, and which they flatter themſelves will merit a degree of public approbation equal to the former.

A great variety of admired Scots and Iriſh airs are here introduced, which the nature of our plan prevented us from inserting in the former work; and, to render this volume a fit sequel to the first, it is also enriched with the latest and most admired songs of Dibdin, Hook, and other celebrated Composers.

CONTENTS.

A
	Page.
A scarlet coat and white cockade	46
Anacreon, they say, was a jolly old blade	76
At the peaceful midnight hour	84
As down on Banna's banks I stray'd	131
As Jamie Gay gaed blithe his way	140
At Beauty's shrine I long have bow'd	184
A sailor's life 's a life of woe	186
Assist me, ye lads	218
Ask if yon damask rose be sweet	240
An gin ye meet a bonny lassie	271
Ah! why must words my flame reveal	274
Adieu ye groves	276
Adieu, adieu my only life	322
At Polwart on the green	334
As I came by Loch Eroch side	358

B
Blow, blow thou winter's wind	38
By moonlight on the green	74
Busk ye, busk ye, my bonny bride	108
By Pinkie house	138
Behold the man that is unlucky	322
By a murmuring stream	332
Blest as th' immortal gods is he	336

	Page
By smooth winding Tay	338
Betty early gone a maying	354

C

Come sing round my favourite tree	24
Chloe, by that borrowed kiss	69
Come now, all ye social powers	236
Come, rouse from your trances	244
Come rouse, brother sportsman	253
Cotchelin sat all alone	318

D

Dear is my little native vale	60
Down the burn, and through the mead	158
Dunbarton's drums beat bonny, O	204
Dear Roger, if your Jenny geck	273
Diogenes, surly and proud	294
Dear image of the maid I love	311

E

Eac fluent bard replete with wit	79
Encompass'd in angel's frame	112

F

Flow, thou regal purple stream	17
For tenderness form'd	26

	Page
Faireſt of the virgin train	110
For ever Fortune	134
From the eaſt breaks the morn	222
From the chace in the mountain	297

H

Here, a ſheer hulk, lies poor Tom Bowling	36
How bleſt has my time been	82
How bleſt the maid	128
Had I a heart for falſhood fram'd	130
How ſtands the glaſs around	202
How ſweetly ſmells the ſimmer green	222
Here awa, there awa	330
Hark, Phillis, hark	369

I

I ſing the Britiſh ſoldier's praiſe	51
John met with Peg the other day	56
I loo'd ne'er a laddie but ane	67
I ſail'd from the Downs	91
In winter when the rain ran'd cauld	152
I that once was a ploughman	196
I winna marry ony man	232
In wine there is all in this life	256
I made love to Kate	258
I've found out a gift for my fair	262
If to force me to ſing	268
In former times we France did rout	308
Jack Ratlin was the ableſt ſeaman	320
In this ſad and ſilent gloom	360

L

	Page
Let bards elate, of Sue and Kate	162
Let gay ones and great	224
Love's goddess, in a myrtle grove	278
Life's like a ship	299
Look where my dear Hamilia smiles	340
Love never more shall give me pain	344

M

My days have been so wond'rous free	33
My laddie is gane far away o'er the plain	62
Must peace and pleasure's melting strain	116
My lodging is on the cold ground	146
My daddie is a canker'd carle	228
My Colin leaves fair London town	238

N

Never till now I knew love's smart	250
Now's the time for mirth and glee	251
Now Phœbus sinketh in the west	264

O

Our trade to work in clay began	94
On sturdy stout Dobbin	96
O thou lov'd country	102
Once more I'll tune the vocal shell	104

	Page
O fee that form that faintly gleams	107
O'er moorlands and mountains	155
O why should old age	206
Old care begone	247
O waly, waly, up yon bank	328
O Logie o' Buchan	364

P

Pain'd with her flighting Jamie's love	362

S.

See, fee the jolly god appears	31
Soft Zephyrs, in thy balmy wing	99
Sweet ditties would my Patty fing	114
Shepherds, I have loft my love	136
Still the lark finds repofe	144
Sweet doth blush the rofy morning	170
Say, have you in the village feen	172
Sweet Annie frae the fea-beach came	174
Some talk of Alexander	211
Says Plato, why should man be vain	226
Says Colin to me	260
Saw ye nae my Peggy	346

T

Though Bacchus may boaft	13
'Twas Saturday's night	21
The meadows look chearful	28

	Page
The hardy sailor braves the ocean	29
The wind was hush'd	40
Thy fatal shafts unerring move	58
To the winds, to the waves	70
Thus, thus, my boys, our anchor's weigh'd	72
Thou'rt gone awa, thou'rt gone awa	120
The heavy hours are almost past	122
The summer was over	124
The morn was fair	126
'Twas summer, and softly	148
Tight lads have I sail'd with	190
There was a jolly millar	209
The echoing horn	214
The fields were green	216
There was a little man	266
The dusky night	283
To ease his heart, and own his flame	289
'Twas within a mile of Edinburgh	306
The fields were gay	313
To Batchelor's hall	315
There's nought but care on ev'ry han'	352
Tho' distant far from Jessy's charms	356
The spring time returns	370

W

Were I oblig'd to beg my bread	43
Whilst happy in my native land	48
We bipeds, made up of frail clay	44
Why tarries my love	54

	Page
Why, don't you know me by my scars?	64
When innocent pastime	88
When summer comes	142
Whene'er I think on that dear spot	160
When I think on this world's pelf	164
When Phœbus first salutes the east	196
When airy dreams	168
When merry hearts were gay	176
Willie was a wanton wag	179
When morn her sweets	182
Won't you hail the leap year	193
When Cupid holds the myrtle crown	200
With an honest old friend	225
When fragrant bloom of yellow broom	230
When late I wander'd	234
Why hangs that cloud upon thy brow	280
When Orpheus went down	292
While here Anacreon's chosen sons	301
Whilst some for pleasure pawn their health	326
When I was at home	342
Will ye gang o'er the lee-rig	348
What numbers shall the muse repeat	350

Y

Ye mortals whom fancies	242
Ye gales that gently wave the sea	263
You're welcome to Paxton	304
Young Peggy blooms our bonniest lass	360

THE EDINBURGH MUSICAL MISCELLANY.

SONG I.

THO' BACCHUS MAY BOAST OF HIS CARE-KILLING BOWL.

SUNG BY MR BOWDEN.

Tho' Bacchus may boaſt of his care-killing bowl, And Folly in thought-drowning revels de-light, Such worſhip a-las! hath no charms for the ſoul, When ſofter devotions the ſenſes

in-vite : When softer devotions the sen - ses
invite. To the arrow of fate, or the canker
of care, His potions oblivious a balm may be-
stow : But to Fancy, that feeds on the charms
of the fair, The death of reflection's the birth
of all woe : The death of reflection's the birth
of all woe.

What foul that's poffeft of a dream fo divine,
  With riot would bid the fweet vifion begone?
For the tear that bedews Senfibility's fhrine
  Is a drop of more worth than all Bacchus's tun.

Is a drop of more worth than all Bacchus's tun.

The tender excefs which enamours the heart,
  To few is imparted, to millions deny'd;
'Tis the brain of the victim that tempers the dart,
  And fools jeft at that for which fages have died.
    And fools, &c.

Each change and excefs hath through life been my
    doom,
  And well can I fpeak of its joy and its ftrife;
The bottle affords us a glimpfe thro' the gloom,
  But love's the true funfhine that gladdens our life.
    But love's, &c.

Come then, rofy Venus, and fpread o'er my fight
  The magic illufions that ravifh the foul:
Awake in my breaft the foft dream of delight,
  And drop from thy myrtle one leaf in my bowl.
    And drop, &c.

Then deep will I drink of the nectar divine,
　Nor e'er, jolly God, from thy banquet remove,
But each tube of my Heart ever thirst for the wine,
　That's mellow'd by friendship, and sweeten'd by love.

That's mellow'd by friendship, and sweeten'd by love.

☞ *The above Notes are trifling deviations from the original melody, to suit the expression of the different stanzas.*

SONG II.

FLOW THOU REGAL PURPLE STREAM.

Flow thou regal purple ſtream, Tincted by
the ſolar beam; In my goblet ſparkling riſe,
Cheer my heart, and glad my eyes: Flow thou
re-gal purple ſtream, Tincted by the ſolar beam; In my gob--let ſpark-ling riſe,
Cheer my heart and glad my eyes: In my

sparkling goblet rife, Cheer my heart and glad my eyes, Cheer my heart, and glad my eyes. My brain afcend on Fancy's wing, 'Noint me wine, a jovial king: My brain afcend on Fancy's wing, 'Noint me, wine, a jo-vial king: My brain afcend on Fancy's wing, 'Noint me, wine, a jovial king, 'Noint me, wine, a jo-

MUSICAL MISCELLANY. 19

vial king, a jo- - - - - - - - - - - - - - -

- -

- -vial king, a jovial king, a jovial king.

While I live, I'll lave my clay ; When I'm dead

and gone away, Let my thirsty subjects say, A

month he reign'd, and that was May: While

I live, I'll lave my clay; When I'm dead, and

gone away, Let my thirsty subjects say, A month

he reign'd, but that was May: Let my thirsty

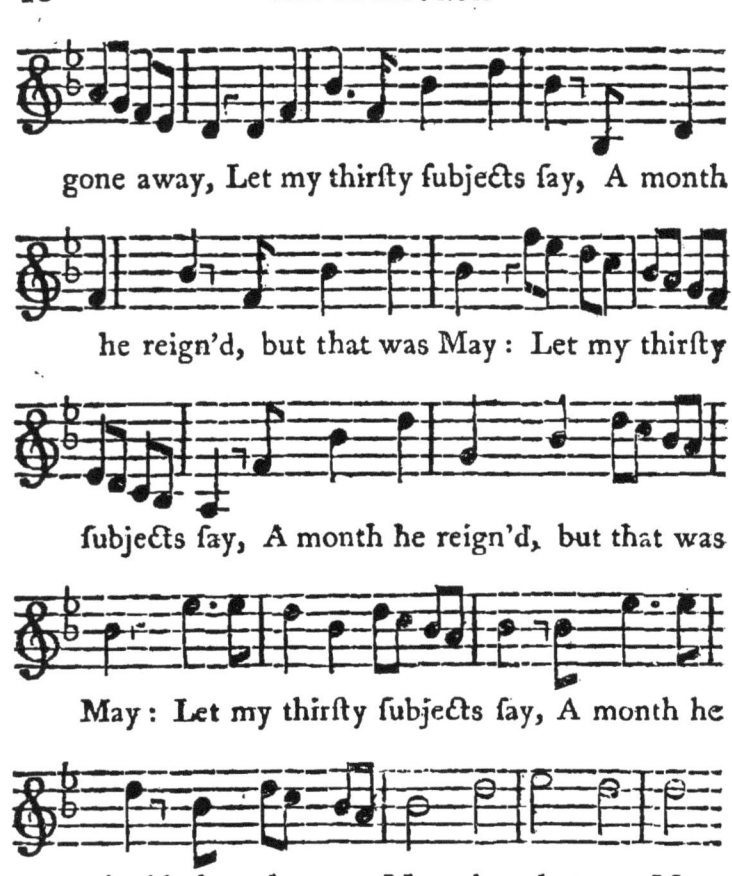

subjects say, A month he reign'd, but that was

May: Let my thirsty subjects say, A month he

reign'd, but that was May, but that was May,

but that was May.

SONG III.

SATURDAY NIGHT AT SEA.

'Twas Saturday night, the twinkling stars

Shone on the rippling sea: No duty call'd the

jo-vial tars, The helm was lash'd a--lee,

The helm was lash'd a--lee. The am-ple

can adorn'd the board, Prepar'd to see it

out, Each gave the lass that he a---dor'd

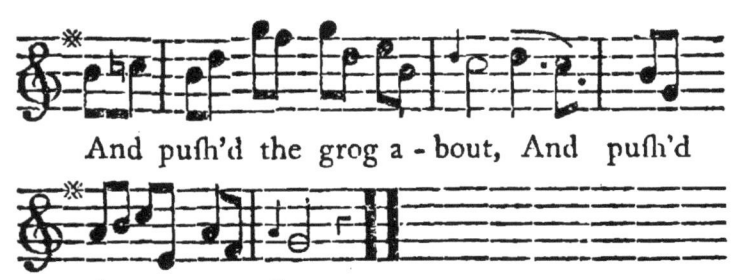

And puſh'd the grog a-bout, And puſh'd the grog a--bout.

Cried honeſt Tom, my Peg I'll toaſt,
   A frigate neat and trim,
All jolly Portſmouth's favourite boaſt :
   I'd venture life and limb,
Sail ſeven long years, and ne'er ſee land,
   With dauntleſs heart and ſtout,
So tight a veſſel to command :
   Then puſh the grog about.

I'll give, cried little Jack, my Poll,
   Sailing in comely ſtate,
Top ga'nt-ſails ſet ſhe is ſo tall,
   She looks like a firſt-rate.
Ah! would ſhe take her Jack in tow,
   A voyage for life throughout,
No better birth I'd wiſh to know :
   Then puſh the grog about.

I'll give, cried I, my charming Nan,
   Trim, handſome, neat, and tight.
What joy, ſo neat a ſhip to man !
   Oh! ſhe's my heart's delight.

So well she bears the storms of life,
  I'd sail the world throughout,
Brave every toil for such a wife;
  Then push the grog about.

Thus to describe Poll, Peg, or Nan,
  Each his best manner tried,
Till summon'd by the empty can,
  They to their hammocks hied:
Yet still did they their vigils keep,
  Though the huge can was out;
For in soft visions gentle sleep
  Still push'd the grog about.

SONG IV.

COME SING ROUND MY FAVOURITE TREE.

Come, fing round my fa-vou-rite tree, Ye fongfters that vifit the grove; 'Twas the haunt of my fhepherd and me, And the bark is a re-cord of love. Sing round my fa-vou-rite treee: Come, ye fongfters that vifit the grove, 'Twas the haunt of my fhepherd and me, 'Twas the haunt of my shepherd and me, And the

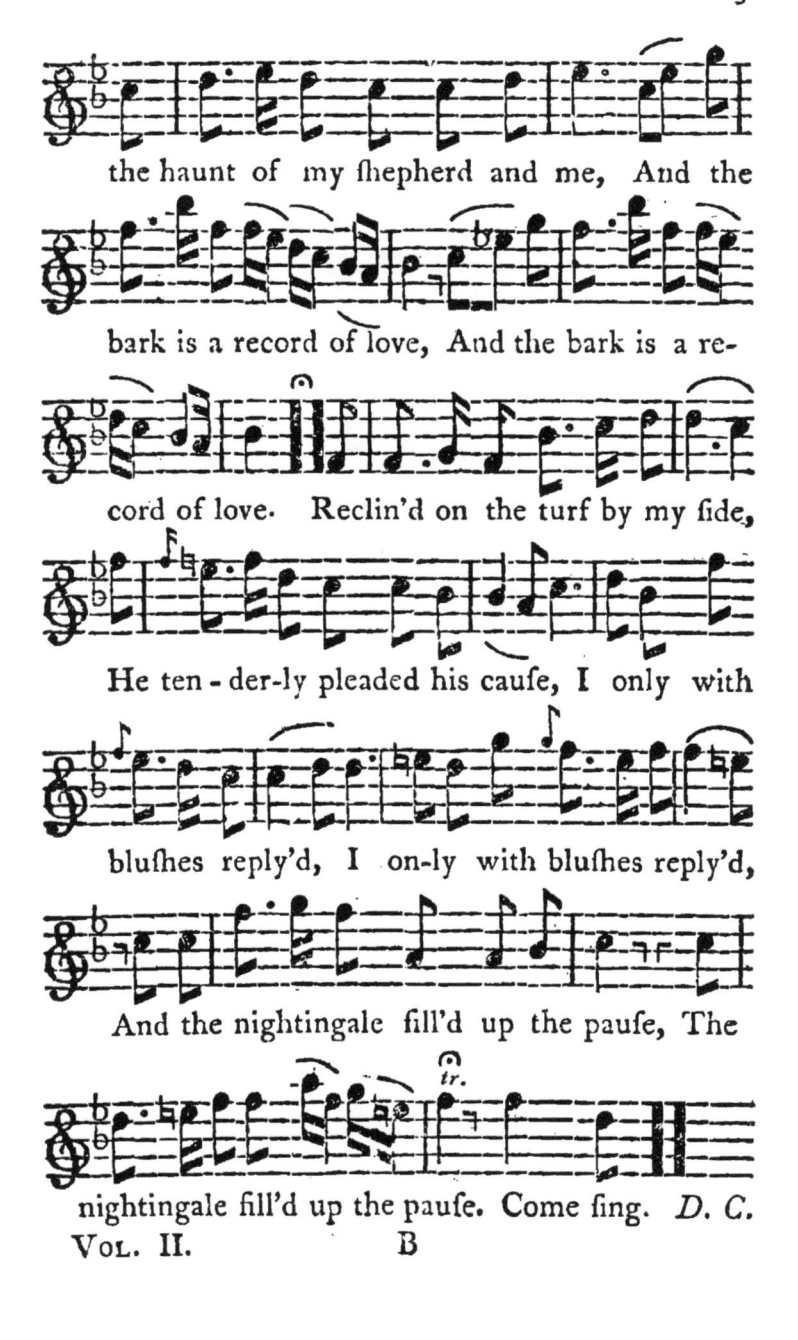

bark is a record of love, And the bark is a re-

cord of love. Reclin'd on the turf by my side,

He ten-der-ly pleaded his cause, I only with

blushes reply'd, I on-ly with blushes reply'd,

And the nightingale fill'd up the pause, The

nightingale fill'd up the pause. Come sing. *D. C.*

SONG V.

FOR TENDERNESS FORM'D.

For tendernefs form'd in life's early day,

A parent's foft forrows to mine led the way,

A parent's foft forrows to mine led the way.

The leffon of pi-ty was caught from

her eye, And ere words were my own I

fpoke with a figh.

The nightingale plunder'd, the mate widow'd dove,
The warbled complaint of the suffering grove,
To youth as it ripen'd gave sentiment new,
The object still changing, the sympathy true.

Soft embers of passion, yet rest in the glow,
A warmth of more pain may this breast never know!
Or, if too indulgent the blessing I claim,
Let the spark drop from reason that wakens the flame.

SONG VI.

THE LASSES OF DUBLIN.

The meadows look cheerful, the birds sweetly sing, So gayly they carrol the praises of spring! Tho' Nature rejoices, poor Norah shall mourn, Until her dear Patrick again shall return. Tho' gain shall return.

Ye Lasses of Dublin, ah, hide your gay charms,
Nor lure her dear Patrick from Norah's fond arms:
Tho' sattins, and ribbons, and laces are fine,
They hide not a heart with such feeling as mine.

SONG VII.

THE HARDY SAILOR.

The hardy sailor braves the ocean, Fearless of the roaring wind; Yet his heart, with soft e-mo-tion, Throbs to leave his love be-hind: Throbs, throbs, throbs, throbs: Yet his heart, with soft e--mo--tion, throbs To leave his love be-hind --- To leave his

30 THE EDINBURGH

love be-hind - - - - - - - - - - - - - - - - To

leave, to leave his love behind. To

dread of foreign foes a stranger, Tho' the

youth can dauntless roam, Alarming fears paint

ev'-ry danger, In a rival left at home: A-

larming fears paint ev'ry danger In a ri-

val left at home - - - - - - - - - - The. *D.C.*

MUSICAL MISCELLANY. 31

SONG VIII.
PRECIOUS GOBLET.

See the jol-ly jol---ly god appears, In--his hand the bowl he rears, Quaffing let me drown my cares, And all---thy no--ble fpirit fhare Pre--cious gob-let, cup divine, Let me, let me quaff thy rofy wine: Pre---cious gob--let, cup divine, Let me *let me quaff thy ro-fy wine.*

Let my hoary honours grow,
Wrinkles trefpafs on my brow;
Let them come, prepar'd I ftand,
And grafp my goblet in my hand.
   Precious goblet, &c.

Cupid, in my youthful hour,
Led me captive of his pow'r,
Now, with branches from the vine,
I guard me from his dart divine.
   Precious goblet, &c.

Bacchus! jolly God, appear!
None but choiceft fouls are here,
Pierce thy oldeft, deepeft cafk,
And let us drain the frequent flafk.
   Precious goblet, &c.

SONG IX.

MY DAYS HAVE BEEN SO WOND'ROUS FREE.

My days have been so wond'rous free, The little birds that fly, With careless ease, from tree to tree, Were but as blest as I. Ask glid-ing wa-ters, if a tear Of mine encreas'd their stream; Or ask the passing gales, if e'er I lent a sigh to them: Or ask the passing gales, If e'er I lent a sigh to them. But now

my former days retire, And I'm by beauty

caught: The tender chains of soft desire are

fix'd upon my thought: An ea-ger hope, with-

in my breast, Does every doubt controul,

And love-ly Bet-sy stands confest the fav'rite

of my soul.

Ye nightingales, ye twifting pines,
    Ye fwains that haunt the grove,
Ye gentle echoes, breezy winds,
    Ye clofe retreats of love.
With all of nature, all of art,
    Affift the dear defign.
O teach a young unpractis'd heart
    To make her ever mine.

The very thought of change I hate,
    As much as of defpair!
And hardly covet to be great,
    Unlefs it be for her.
'Tis true, the paffion of my mind
    Is mixt with foft diftrefs;
Yet while the fair I love is kind,
    I cannot wifh it lefs.

But if fhe treats me with difdain,
    And flights my well-meant love,
Or looks with pleafure on my pain,
    A pain fhe wont remove;
Farewell, ye birds, and lonely pines,
    Adieu to groans and fighs.
I'll leave my paffion to the winds,
    Love unreturn'd foon dies.

N. B. *The Second and Third Stanzas muft be fung to the laft Air, and the Fourth Stanza to the Former.*

SONG X.

POOR TOM, OR THE SAILOR'S EPITAPH.

Here, a ſheer hulk, lies poor Tom Bowling, The darling of our crew; No more he'll hear the tempeſt howling, For death has broach'd him to. His form was of the manlieſt beauty, His heart was kind and ſoft; Faithful below he did his du-ty,

And now he's gone a - - - loft, And now he's gone a - - loft.

Tom never from his word departed,
  His virtues were so rare,
His friends were many, and true-hearted,
  His Poll was kind and fair:
And then he'd sing so blithe and jolly,
  Ah many's the time and oft!
But mirth is turn'd to melancholy,
  For Tom is gone aloft.

Yet shall Poor Tom find pleasant weather,
  When he who all commands,
Shall give, to call life's crew together,
  The word to pipe all hands.
Thus death, who kings and tars dispatches,
  In vain Tom's life has doff'd;
For, tho' his body's under hatches,
  His soul is gone aloft.

SONG XI.

BLOW, BLOW, THOU WINTER'S WIND.

Blow, blow, thou winter's wind, Thou art
not so unkind, thou art not so unkind, As
men's in-gra-ti-tude: Thy tooth is not so
keen, Because thou art not seen; Thy tooth
is not so keen, Because thou art not seen;
Altho' thy breath be rude, Altho' thy breath

be rude, Al-tho' thy breath be rude.

Freeze, freeze, thou bitter ſky,
Thou doſt not bite ſo nigh
    As benefit forgot:
Tho' thou the waters warp,
Thy ſting is not ſo ſharp
    As friend remember'd not.

SONG XII.

BUXOM NAN.

The wind was hufh'd, the ſtorm was over,

Unfurl'd was e - - very flowing fail, From toil

releas'd, when Dick of Dover Went with his

meſsmates to re-gale. All danger's o'er, cried

he, my neathearts, Drown care, then, in the

ſmiling can: Come, bear a hand, let's toaſt

our sweethearts, And first I'll give my buxom Nan: Come, bear a hand, let's toast our sweethearts, And first I'll give my buxom Nan, First I'll give my buxom Nan.

She's none of they that's always gigging,
    And stem and stern made up of art;
One knows a vessel by her rigging,
    Such ever flight a constant heart.

With straw-hat, and pink-streamers flowing,
    How oft to meet me has she ran;
While for dear life would I be rowing,
    To meet with smiles my buxom Nan.

Jack Jollyboat went to the Indies,
    To see him stare when he came back,

The girls were so all off the hinges,
   His Poll was quite unknown to Jack.

Tant masted all, to see who's tallest,
   Breast works, top-ga'nt sails, and a fan;
Messmate, cried I, more sail than ballast,
   Ah still give me my buxom Nan.

None on life's sea can sail more quicker,
   To shew her love, or serve a friend:
But hold, I'm preaching o'er my liquor,
   This one word more, and there's an end.

Of all the wenches whatsomever,
   I say, then, find me out who can,
One half so true, so kind, so clever,
   Sweet, trim, and neat, as buxom Nan.

SONG XII.

SOMEBODY.

Were I oblig'd to beg my bread, And had not where to lay my head, I'd creep where yonder herds are fed, And steal a look at somebody, My own dear somebody, my constant somebody, I'd creep where yonder herds are fed, and steal a look at some-bo-dy.

When I'm laid low, and am at reft,
And maybe number'd with the bleft,
Oh! may thy artlefs feeling breaft
Throb with regard for—Somebody:
Ah! will you drop the pitying tear,
And figh for the loft—Somebody?

But fhould I ever live to fee
That form fo much ador'd by me,
Then thou'lt reward my conftancy,
And I'll be bleft with—Somebody:
Then fhall my tears be dried by thee,
And I'll be bleft with—Somebody.

SONG XIII.

WHILST HAPPY IN MY NATIVE LAND.

Whilft happy in my native land, I boaft my country's charter, I'll never bafely lend my hand, Her liberties to bar-ter. The noble mind is not at all By poverty degraded, 'Tis

guilt alone can make us fall, And well I am

perſuaded, Each free-born Briton's ſong ſhould

be, Or give me death or liberty, or give me

death or liberty, or give me death or liberty,

or give me death or liberty.

Tho' ſmall the pow'r which fortune grants,
  And few the gifts ſhe ſends us,
The lordly hireling often wants
  That freedom which defends us.

By law fecur'd from lawlefs ftrife,
  Our houfe is our caftellum;
Thus blefs'd with all that's dear in life,
  For lucre fhall we fell them?
    No:—ev'ry Briton's fong fhould be,
  Or give me death or liberty, &c.

SONG XIV.

THE VOLUNTEER.

A fcarlet coat, and fmart cockade, Are pafports to the fair; For Venus felf was kind, 'tis faid, To Mars the God of war. Then, fince my  country calls to arms, Love's livery will I wear;

MUSICAL MISCELLANY. 47

Nor seek reward save Nanny's charms, But go a volunteer, but go a volunteer, but go a volunteer; Nor seek reward save Nanny's charms, But go a volunteer, Nor seek reward save Nanny's charms, but go a volunteer.

Should fortune smile, and grant me fame,
    The laurel will be thine,
The flowers of love I only claim,
    Ah! let their sweets entwine.
        Then since my country calls to arms,
            Love's liv'ry will I wear,
        Nor seek reward save Nanny's charms,
            But go a volunteer.

All hardships seem as light as air,
While British maids we guard,
Each soldier has one darling care,
Her smiles his best reward.
 Then since my country calls to arms,
 Love's liv'ry will I wear,
 Nor seek reward save Nanny's charms,
 But go a volunteer.

SONG XV.

SOUND ARGUMENT.

We bipeds made up of frail clay, Alas are the children of sorrow; And tho' brisk and merry to-day, We all may be wretched to-morrow: For sunshine's succeeded by rain,

Then fearful of life's stormy weather, Left pleasure should only bring pain: Let us all be unhappy together, let us all be unhappy together, let us all be unhappy together, For sunshine's succeeded by rain. Then, fearful of life's stormy weather, Left pleasure should on-ly bring pain, Let us all be unhappy together.

I grant, the beſt bleſſing we know
   Is a friend---for true friendſhip's a treaſure,
And yet, left your friend prove a foe,
   Oh taſte not the dangerous pleaſure.
Thus friendſhip's a flimſy affair ;
   Thus riches and health are a bubble ;
Thus there's nothing delightful but care,
   Nor any thing pleaſing but trouble.

If a mortal would point out that life,
   That on earth could be neareſt to heaven,
Let him, thanking his ſtars, chooſe a wife,
   To whom truth and honour are given :
But honour and truth are ſo rare,
   And horns, when they're cutting, ſo tingle,
That with all my reſpect for the fair,
   I'd adviſe him to ſigh and live ſingle.

It appears from theſe premiſes plain,
   That wiſdom is nothing but folly,
That pleaſure's a term that means pain,
   And that joy is your true melancholy.
That all thoſe who laugh ought to cry,
   That 'tis fine friſk and fun to be grieving ;
And that, ſince we muſt all of us die,
   We ſhould all be unhappy while living.

SONG XVII.

THE NEGLECTED SOLDIER.

IN ANSWER TO THE NEGLECTED TAR.

I sing the British soldier's praise, A theme  renown'd in story, It well deserves more polish'd  lays, Oh 'tis your boast and glory. When  thund'ring Mars spreads war around, By them  you are protected; But when in peace the nation's found, Poor souls they are neglected. But

oh! stretch forth your aiding hand, in to-ken
of their merit, Then boldly they'll march o'er 
the land, And shew a grateful spirit. 

For you the musket first he takes,
   That you may rest in quiet,
His wife and children he forsakes,
   To shift for cloaths and diet.
He's sudden call'd, he knows not where,
   Nor knows he shall return
To those he left in deep despair,
   Whose hearts for him yet burn.
But oh! stretch forth your bounteous hand,
   In justice to their merit,
Then cheerful they'll march through the land,
   And shew a grateful spirit.

For you through many a tedious road
   He goes without complaining,
From scorching heat he seeks abode,
   Sometimes without obtaining :

By thirſt and hunger oft he's preſt,
　Yet ſcorns to droop his head,
Ambition from within his breaſt
　He ſubſtitutes as bread.
Then oh! ſtretch forth your friendly hand,
　In juſtice to his merit,
How cheerful he'll march through the land,
　And bleſs your gen'rous ſpirit!

For you through fields of blood they'll ſeek
　Your foes of ev'ry nation;
'Tis there bold actions loudly ſpeak
　Their worth in ev'ry ſtation.
Firm as a flinty wall they'll ſtand,
　Obſerving ſtrict decorum,
Until their leader gives command
　To beat down all before 'em.
Then oh! ſtretch forth th' aſſiſting hand,
　In juſtice to their merit,
When they return unto their land,
　They'll bleſs your noble ſpirit.

Well, now they've threſh'd the foe, we'll ſay,
　Did all within their power,
But little more than blows have they,
　And one farthing an hour.
Little within the Frenchman's fob
　To recompenſe their labours;
Why then it proves a ſorry job,
　Little better than their neighbours.

Then oh! stretch forth the lib'ral hand,
　In justice to their merit,
So shall they bless their happy land,
　The land of godlike spirit.

SONG XVIII.

THE PIDGEON.

Why tarries my love? Ah! where does he rove? My love is long absent from me -- Come hither, my dove, I'll write to my love, And send him a let--ter by thee--- And fend him a let-ter by thee.

  To find him swift fly,
  The letter I'll tye
Secure to thy leg with a string:
  Ah! not to my leg,
  Fair lady I beg,
But fasten it under my wing.

  Her dove she did deck,
  She drew o'er his neck
A bell and a collar so gay;
  She ty'd to his wing
  The scroll with a string,
Then kiss'd him and sent him away.

  It blew and it rain'd,
  The pidgeon disdain'd
To seek shelter, undaunted he flew;
  'Till wet was his wing,
  And painful the string,
So heavy the letter it grew.

  He flew all around,
  'Till Colin he found,
Then perch'd on his hand with the prize;
  Whose heart while he reads,
  With tenderness bleeds
For the pigeon,---that flutters---and dies!

SONG XIX.

LOVE AND TIME.

John met with Peg the other day, As she to church was walking; And as he had a deal to say, He straight began a-talking, a-talking, a--talking, He straight be-gan a-talking. He ask'd her if her heart was free, Or if she him ap--prov'd-- And all the while could plainly see Her snowy bosom mov'd,

--- Her snowy bo-som mov'd.

His heart was yet 'tween hope and fear,
  And strove his thoughts to smother;
Unless those heavings of his dear
  Perchance were for some other.
A while she blush'd, and now she smil'd,
  Cry'd, pr'ythee be not simple;
When love the more his heart beguil'd,
  And sported in each dimple.

She thought he talk'd too soon of love---
  'Twas time enough for wooing:
He told her time would swiftly move,
  And time was love's undoing.
Peg then replied: If that's the case,
  'Tis time that we were moving;
And said, with sadness in her face,
  He sure won't kill for loving.

Why then, cried John, let's haste to church,
  And all our fears deliver;

Old time shall linger in the lurch,
   And love shall live for ever.
Away they went, made most of time,
   In spite of all his flurry;
Love saw they both were in their prime,
   And join'd them in a hurry.

SONG XX.

THY FATAL SHAFTS UNERRING MOVE.

Thy fatal shafts un-err-ing move, I bow before thine al-tar, Love: I feel the soft re-sistless flame Glide swift through all my vi-tal frame.

For while I gaze my bosom glows,
My blood in tides impetuous flows;
Hope, fear, and joy, alternate roll,
And floods of transport whelm my soul.

My fault'ring tongue attempts in vain,
In soothing numbers to complain;
My tongue some secret magic ties,
My murmurs sink in broken sighs.

Condemn'd to nurse eternal care,
And ever drop this silent tear;
Unheard I mourn, unknown I sigh,
Unfriended live, unpitied die.

SONG XX.

DEAR IS MY LITTLE NATIVE VALE.

Dear is my little native vale, The ring-dove builds and warbles there, Close by my cote she tells her tale To every passing vil-la-ger: The squirrel leaps from tree to tree, And shells his nuts at liberty.

In orange groves, and myrtle bow'rs,
That breathe a gale of fragrance round,
I charm the fairy footed hours,
With my lov'd lute's romantic sound.

Or crowns of living laurel weave
For thofe that win the race at eve.

The fhepherds horn, at break of day,
The ballet danc'd at twilight glade,
The canzonet, and roundelay,
Sung in the filent greenwood fhade:
Thefe fimple joys, that never fail,
Shall bind me to my native vale.

SONG XXI.

JOCKEY.

My lad-die is gang'd far a--way o'er the plain, Where in for-row behind I'm forc'd to remain: Tho' blue-bells and vi'—lets the hedges adorn; Tho' trees are in blofiom, and fweet blows the thorn, No pleafure they give me, in vain they look gay, There's nothing can pleafe now, my Jockey's away, Forlorn I fit

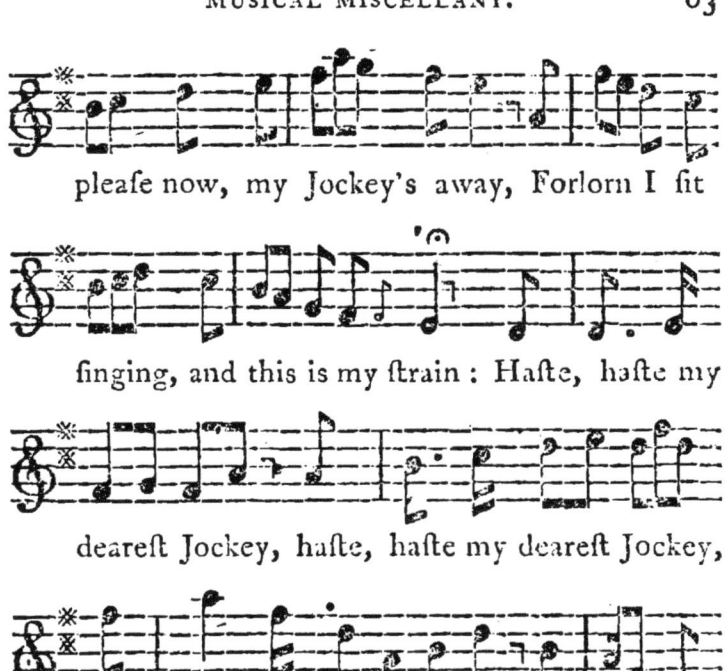

finging, and this is my ftrain: Hafte, hafte my

deareft Jockey, hafte, hafte my deareft Jockey,

Hafte, hafte, my deareft Jockey, to me back

a - - gain.

When the lads and their laffes are on the green met,
They dance and they fing, they laugh and they chat;
Contented and happy, their hearts full of glee,
I can't without envy their merriment fee:
Thofe paftimes offend me, my Shepherd's not there,
No pleafure I relifh that Jockey don't fhare;
It makes me to figh, I from tears fcarce refrain,
I wifh my dear Jockey return'd back again.

But hope fhall fuftain me, nor will I defpair;
He promis'd he would in a fortnight be here;
On fond expectation my wifhes I'll feaft,
For Love my dear Jockey to Jenny will hafte.
Then farewell, each care, and adieu each vain figh,
Who'll then be fo bleft or fo happy as I:
I'll fing on the meadows, and alter my ftrain,
When Jockey returns to my arms back again.

SONG XXII.

SOLDIER DICK.

Why, don't you know me by my fcars?
I'm fol-dier Dick come from the wars, Where
many a head with-out a hat Crowd honour's
bed: but what of that? Crowd honour's bed:

MUSICAL MISCELLANY. 65

but what of that? Beat drums, play fifes, 'tis

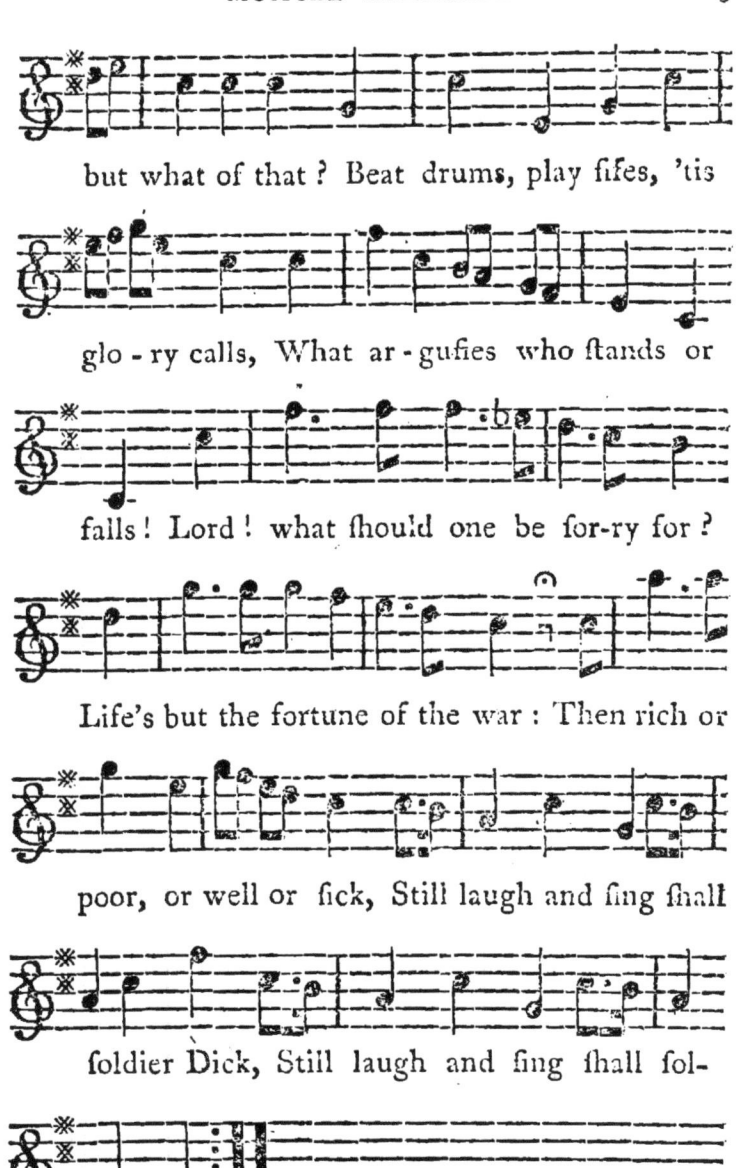

glo-ry calls, What ar-gufies who ſtands or

falls! Lord! what ſhould one be for-ry for?

Life's but the fortune of the war: Then rich or

poor, or well or ſick, Still laugh and ſing ſhall

ſoldier Dick, Still laugh and ſing ſhall fol-

dier Dick.

I used to look two ways at once,
A bullet hit me on the sconce,
And doush'd my eye---d'ye think I'd wince !
Why, Lord ! I've never squinted since.
  Beat drums, &c.

Some distant keep from war's alarms,
For fear of wooden legs and arms ;
While others die safe in their beds,
Who all their lives had wooden heads.
  Beat drums, &c.

Thus gout or fever, sword or shot,
Or something sends us all to pot :
That we're to die, then, do not grieve,
But let's be merry while we live.
  Beat drums, &c.

SONG XXIII.

I LO'ED NE'ER A LADDIE BUT ANE.

I lo'ed ne'er a laddie but ane, He lo'ed ne'er a laſſie but me; He is willing to mak' me his ain, And his ain I am willing to be. He has coft me a rocklay o' blue, And a pair o' mit-tins o' green: The price was a kiſs o' my mou' And I paid him the debt yeſtreen.

Let ithers brag weel o' their gear,
   Their land, and their lordly degree
I carena for ought but my dear,
   For he's ilka thing lordly to me:
His words mair than sugar are sweet,
   His sense drives ilk fear far awa';
I listen, poor fool! and I greet,
   Yet, oh! how sweet are the tears as they fa'!

" Dear lassie," he cries wi' a jeer,
   " Ne'er heed what the auld anes will say;
" Tho' we've little to brag o', ne'er fear,
   " What's gowd to a heart that is wae?
" Our laird has baith honours and wealth,
   " Yet see! how he's dwining wi' care;
" Now we, tho' we've naithing but health,
   " Are cantie and leil evermair.

" O Menie! the heart that is true,
   " Has something mair costly than gear,
" Ilk e'en it has has naithing to rue,
   " Ilk morn it has naithing to fear.
" Ye wardlings! gae hoard up your store,
   " And tremble for fear ought ye tyne:
" Guard your treasures wi' lock, bar, and door,
   " While thus in my arms I lock mine."

He ends wi' a kiss and a smile,
   Waes me! can I take it amiss,

When a lad, fae unpractis'd in guile,
  Smiles saftly, and ends wi' a kiss!
Ye lasses, wha lo'e to torment
  Your lemans wi' fause scorn and strife,
Play your pranks,---for I've gi'en my consent,
  And this night I'll take Jamie for life.

SONG XXIV.
CHLOE, BY THAT BORROWED KISS.

Chlo-e, by that borrow'd kiss, I a-las am quite undone! 'Twas so sweet, so fraught with bliss, Thousands will not pay that one! Thou- -sands will not pay that one!

Lest the debt should break your heart,
  (Roguish Chloe, smiling, cries)
Come, a thousand, then, in part,
  For the present shall suffice.

SONG XXV.

AH WELLADAY! MY POOR HEART!

To the winds, to the waves, to the woods I complain, Ah welladay! my poor heart! They hear not my sighs, and they heed not my pain: Ah wel-la-day! my poor heart! Ah welladay! my poor heart!

The name of my goddess I grave on each tree,
    Ah well-a-day my poor heart!
'Tis I wound the bark, but Love's arrows wound me;
    Ah well-a-day my poor heart!

The heavens I view, and their azure-bright skies;
 Ah well-a-day my poor heart!
My heaven exists in her still brighter eyes;
 Ah well-a-day my poor heart!

To the Sun's morning splendor the poor Indinn bows;
 Ah well a-day my poor heart!
But I dare not worship where I pay my vows;
 Ah well-a-day my poor heart!

His God each morn rises, and he can adore;
 Ah well-a-day my poor heart!
But my goddess to me must soon never rise more;
 Ah well a-day my poor heart!

SONG XXVI.

THE SOV'REIGN OF THE SEAS.

Thus, thus my boys, our anchor's weigh'd,

The glorious British flag's display'd, Unfurl'd the

swelling sail: Sound, sound, sound your shells,

ye Tritons, sound, Let ev'-ry heart with joy

rebound, We scud before the gale; Let e-v'ry

heart with joy rebound, We scud be-fore the

gale. For Neptune quits his wa-try car, De-pos'd by Jove's de-cree, Who hails a free-born Britiſh tar the Sov'reign of the ſeas: Who hails a true-born Britiſh tar the ſov'reign of the ſeas, The ſov'reign of the ſeas --- The ſov'-reign of the ſeas.

A ſail a head, our decks we clear,
Our canvas crowd, the chace we near,
 In vain the Frenchman flies:
Vol. II.   F

A broadside pour'd through clouds of smoke,
Our Captain roars, my hearts of Oak,
  Now draw and board your Prize.
    For Neptune, &c.

SONG XXVII.

THE TARTAN PLAIDIE.

By moonlight on the green, Where lads and lasses stray, How sweet the blossom'd bean! How sweet the new made hay! But not to me so sweet The blossoms on the thorn, As when my lad I meet, More fresh than May day morn: Give me the lad so blithe and gay, Give me the Tartan plaidie; For, spite of all the wife can say, I'll wed my Highland laddie: My bonny Highland laddie, My bonny Highland lad-die, My bonny, bonny, bonny, bonny, bonny Highland lad-die.

His skin is white as snow,
  His e'en are bonny blue,
Like rose-bud sweet his mou'
  When wet wi' morning dew,

Young Will is rich and great,
 And fain wou'd ca' me his;
But what is pride or state,
 Without love's smiling Blifs?
  Give me the lad, &c.

When first he talk'd of love,
 He look'd sae blithe and gay,
His flame I did approve,
 And cou'd na say him nay.
Then to the kirk I'll haste,
 There prove my love and truth;
Reward a love sae chaste,
 And wed the constant Youth.
  Give me the lad, &c

SONG XXVIII.

NEW ANACREONTIC SONG.

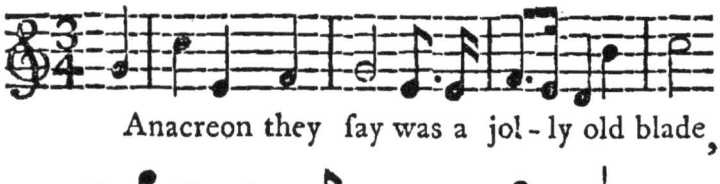

Anacreon they say was a jol-ly old blade,
A Grecian choice spirit, and po-et by trade. A-

nacreon, they say, was a jol---ly old blade, A

Grecian choice spirit, and poet by trade. To

Venus and Bacchus he tun'd up his lays; For

Love and a bumper he sung all his days: To

Venus and Bacchus he tun'd up his lays, For

love and a bumper, For love and a bumper he

sung all his days.

He laugh'd as he quaff'd still the juice of the vine,
And tho' he was human was look'd on divine;
At the feast of good humour he always was there,
And his fancy and sonnets still banish'd dull care.

Good wine, boys, says he, is the liquor of Jove,
'Tis our comfort below and their nectar above;
Then while round the table the bumper we pass,
Let the toast be to Venus and each smiling lass.

Apollo may torment his catgut or wire,
Yet Bacchus and Beauty the theme must inspire,
Or else all his humming and strumming is vain,
The true joys of heaven he'd never obtain.

To love and be lov'd how transporting the bliss,
While the heart-cheering glass gives a zest to each kiss;
With Bacchus and Venus I'll ever combine,
For drinking and kissing are pleasures divine.

As sons of Anacreon then let us be gay,
With drinking and love pass the moments away;
With wine and with beauty let's fill up the span,
For that's the best method, deny it who can.

SONG XXIX.

HEDSOR DALE.

Each fluent bard, replete with wit, In e--qual numbers shines, And smoothly flows some fan-cied name To grace his po-lish'd lines: He calls the Mu--ses to his aid, In verse he tells his am'rous tale. Be thou my muse, thou much lov'd maid, The fair-est

THE EDINBURGH

flow'r of Hed - - - for dale, Of Hed - for dale,

Of Hed - - for dale, Of Hed - - for dale. Be

thou my mufe, thou much lov'd maid, The

faireft flow'r of Hedfor dale.

I feel the warm, the pleafing fire
 Within my bofom roll,
And pureft love and chafte defire
 Steal foftly on my foul:
In vain I wou'd the flame conceal,
 And hide thofe cares my heart affail;
My talk and looks and fighs prevail,
 I love the flow'r of Hedfor Dale!

What pity—that a nymph so fair,
   With winning shape and face,
Should be devoted to some clown,
   Or rustic's rude embrace!
That form demands a better fate;
   Sweet hope, perhaps I can prevail;
I'll try before it is too late,
   To cull the flow'r of Hedsor Dale.

SONG XXX.

HOW BLEST HAS MY TIME BEEN.

How blest has my time been, what joys have I known, Since wedlock's soft bondage made Jes - - -sy my own: So joyful my heart is, so ea-sy my chain, That freedom is tasteless, and rov - - ing a pain.

Thro' walks grown with woodbines as often we stray,
Around us our boys and girls frolic and play:
How pleasing their sport is! the wanton ones see,
And borrow their looks from my Jessy and me.

To try her sweet temper, oft times am I seen,
In revels all day with the nymphs on the green :
Tho' painful my absence, my doubts she beguiles,
And meets me at night with complacence and smiles.

What tho' on her cheeks the rose loses its hue,
Her wit and good humour blooms all the year thro' :
Time still, as he flies, adds increase to her truth,
And gives to her mind what he steals from her youth.

Ye shepherds so gay, who make love to ensnare,
And cheat with false vows the too credulous fair,
In search of true pleasure how vainly you roam,
To hold it for life you must find it at home.

SONG XXXI.

THE WOLF.

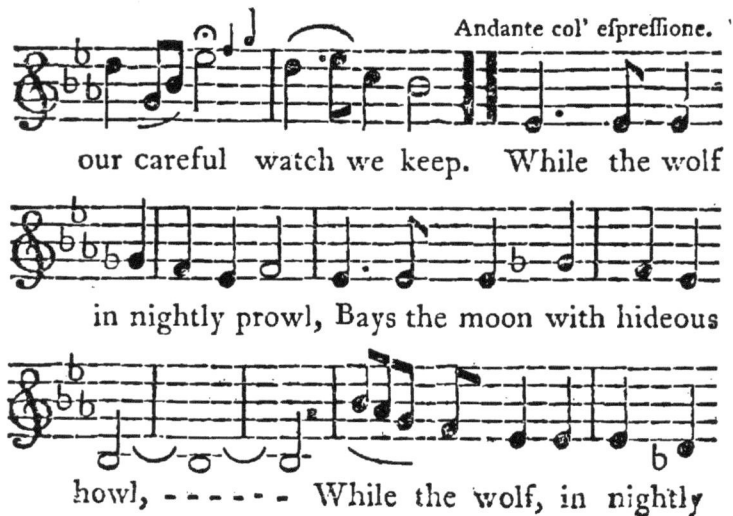

Siciliano.

At the peaceful midnight hour, Every senfe and e-ve-ry power, Fetter'd lies in downy fleep: Then our careful watch we keep, Then

Andante col' efpreffione.

our careful watch we keep. While the wolf in nightly prowl, Bays the moon with hideous howl, - - - - - While the wolf, in nightly prowl, Bays the moon with hideous howl:

While the wolf in nightly prowl, Bays - - - - -

- the moon

Adagio.   Allegro con spirito.

with hideous howl.   Gates are barr'd, a

vain resistance; Females shriek, but no assist-

ance: Silence, silence, or you meet your

fate; Silence, or you meet your fate - - - - -

Vol. II.   G

------ Your keys, your jewels, cash and plate! Your keys, your jewels, your jewels, cash and plate, your jewels, cash and plate, your jewels, cash and plate. Locks, bolts, and bars, soon fly asunder: Locks, bolts, and bars, soon fly asunder, Then to rifle, rob, and plunder: Then to rifle, rob, and plunder

MUSICAL MISCELLANY. 87

Locks, bolts, and bars, soon fly asunder, Then to rifle, rob, and plunder, To rifle, rob, and plunder, To rifle, rob, and plunder.

G 2

88   THE EDINBURGH

SONG XXXII.

JEMMY AND NANNY.

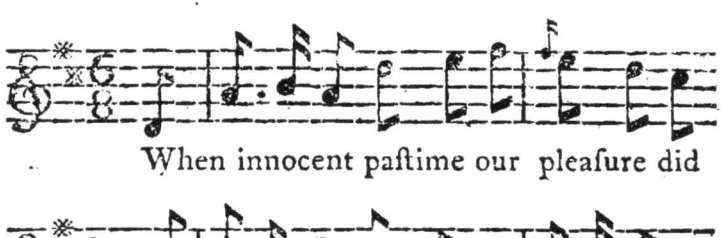

When innocent paſtime our pleaſure did crown, Upon a green meadow, or under a tree; E'er Nanny became a fine lady in town, How lovely and loving and bonny was ſhe! Rouze up thy reaſon, my beautiful Nanny, Let no new whim take thy fan-cy from me: Oh! as thou art bonny, be faithful as o-ny, Favour thy

Jemmy, favour thy Jemmy, favour thy Jemmy

who doats upon thee.

Does the death of a lintwhite give Annie the spleen?
   Can tyning of trifles be uneasy to thee?
Can lap-dogs, or monkies, draw tears from these een?
   That look with indiff'rence on poor dying me!
Rouse up thy reason, my beautiful Annie,
   And dinna prefer a paroquet to me:
O! as thou art bonny, be prudent and canny,
   And think upon Jamie wha doats upon thee.

Ah! should a new mantua, or Flanders-lace head,
   Or yet a wee cotty, tho' never sae fine,
Gar thee grow forgetful, or let his heart bleed,
   That anes had some hope of purchasing thine?
Rouse up thy reason, my beautiful Annie,
   And dinna prefer your fleegaries to me;

O! as thou art bonny, be folid and canny,
    And tent a true lover that doats upon thee.

Shall a Paris-edition of new-fangled Sawny,
    Tho' gilt o'er wi' laces and fringes he be,
By adorning himfelf be admir'd by fair Annie,
    And aim at thofe bennifons promif'd to me:
Roufe up thy reafon, my beautiful Annie,
    And never prefer a light dancer to me:
O! as thou art bonny, be conftant and canny,
    Love only thy Jamie wha doats upon thee.

O think, my dear charmer, on ilka fweet hour,
    That flade awa' faftly between thee and me,
'Ere fquirrels, or beaux, or fopp'ry had pow'r,
    To rival my love, or impofe upon thee.
Roufe up thy reafon, my beautiful Annie,
    And let thy defires be a' center'd in me:
O! as thou art bonny, be faithfu' and canny,
    And love him wha's langing to center in thee.

SONG XXXIV.

THE TAR FOR ALL WEATHERS.

I sail'd from the Downs in the Nancy, my jibb how she smack'd thro' the breeze! She's a vessel quite rigg'd to my fancy, As e'er sail'd on the salt seas: Then adieu to the white cliffs of Britain, Our girls, and our dear native shore, For if some hard rock we should split on, We ne'er should see them a-ny more. But sail-

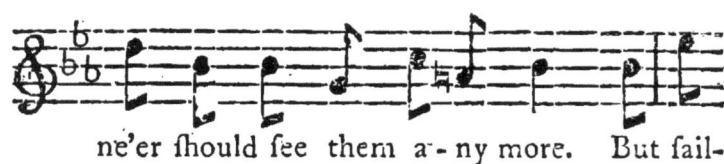

ors are boon for all weathers, Great guns, let

it blow high, blow low! Our duty keeps us

to our tethers, And where the gale drives we

must go.

When we enter'd the gut of Gibralter,
 I verily thought she'd have sunk,
For the wind so began for to alter;
 She yaul'd just as tho' she was drunk.
The squall tore the mainsail to shivers,
 Helm-a-weather the hoarse botswain cries;
Set the foresail a-thwart sea she quivers,
 As through the rough tempest she flies.
  But sailors, &c

The storm came on thicker and faster,
   As black then as pitch was the sky;
But then what a dreadful disaster,
   Befel three poor seamen and I.
Ben Buntlen, Sam Shroud and Dick Handsail,
   By a gale that came furious and hard;
And as we were furling the mainsail,
   We were every soul swept from the yard.
      But sailors, &c.

Poor Ben, Sam and Dick cried peccavi,
   When I at the risk of my neck,
While in peace they sunk down to old Davy,
   Caught a rope and so landed on deck.
Well, what would you have, we were stranded,
   And out of a fine jolly crew,
Of three hundred, that sail'd, never landed,
   But I, and I think, twenty-two.
      But sailors, &c.

At last then at sea having miscarried,
   Another guess way set the wind;
To England I came and got married,
   To a lass that was comely and kind.
But whether for joy or vexation,
   We know not for what we were born;
Perhaps we may find a kind station,
   Perhaps we may touch at Cape Horn.
      But sailors, &c

SONG XXXV.

OUR TRADE TO WORK IN CLAY BEGAN.

Our trade to work in clay began, Ere the
first man was made; For out of clay was made
this man, And thus began our trade. Since man
is but an earthen jug, The jug then let us fill;
For this to empty t'other mug good liquor's
welcome still. In earth, my boys, let's work our

way, And when we're dry, and when we're

dry, we'll wet the clay.

See here a noble chrift'ning bowl,
    But fill it to the brim;
So large, the baby (pretty foul)
    May like young Indians fwim:
The Covent Garden fwell at jupps,
    In this may take his go,
For Afhley's punch houfe here are cups,
    Pro bono publico.
              And when we're dry, &c.

And why abroad our money fling,
    To pleafe our fickle fair,
No more from China, China bring,
    Here's Englifh China ware.
Then, friends, put round the foaming mug,
    And take it with good will,
Since man is but an earthen jug,
    This jug then let us fill.
              And when we're dry, &c.

SONG XXXVI.
THE TWADDLE.

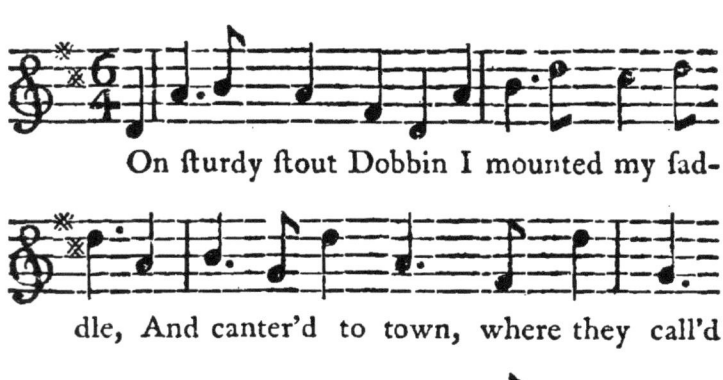

On sturdy stout Dobbin I mounted my saddle, And canter'd to town, where they call'd  me the Twaddle; 'Till I met with a friend by  mere dint of good luck, Who taught me the  Tippee, And now I'm a buck! To swallow six  bottles I now dare engage, Then to knock down those watchmen bent double with age, And if

spent with fatigue to St James's I waddle, To

shew the beau monde I'm no longer the twaddle,

No longer the twaddle, No longer the twaddle,

To shew the beau monde I'm no longer the

twaddle.

Having now learnt to read why I take in the papers,
And draining a bumper to banish the vapours,
I scan the fresh quarrels 'twixt new-married spouses,
To match the debates in both Parliament houses.

Where patriots and placemen keep wrangling for
    fame,
The outs are all faultlefs, the ins are to blame;
Tho' the outs are the Tippee, their brains are all
    addle,
Yet when they get in you foon find 'em the Twaddle.

When Briton's bafe foes dare prefume to unite,
Old Elliot's the Tippee, becaufe he dare fight.
And to poets, who live on the floor next the fky,
Roaft beef is a Tippee they feldom come nigh.
The lawyer and doctor both ftrictly agree
That all is the Twaddle—except 'tis their fee.
And when you from Dover to Calais would ftraddle,
A balloon is the Tippee, a packet's the Twaddle.

Dick Twifting is now quite the Twaddle for tea,
Tho' he once was the Tippee for Green and Bohea;
But then we'd no tax to turn day into night,
No dire Commutation to block up our light.
"Leaft faid's fooneft mended," I hope I'm not wrong;
If I am, pray excufe, and I'll hence hold my tongue:
Perhaps you may think me a mere fiddle faddle,
Yet if not quite the Tippee, don't fay I'm the
    Twaddle.

MUSICAL MISCELLANY. 99

SONG XXXVII.

THE MANSION OF PEACE.

Andante.

Soft zephyr, on thy balmy wing, Thy gentlest breezes hither bring; Her slumbers guard some hand divine, Ah! watch her with a care

Affetuoso.

like mine. A rose! a rose! from her bosom has stray'd; I'll seek to replace it, To replace it with art. A. Art But no, no, no, 'Twill

H 2

her slumbers invade, I'll wear it; fond youth ḃ next my heart. But. heart. A-las! fil-ly rose, fil-ly rose, hadst thou known, 'Twas Daphne that gave thee, that gave thee that place. A place. Thou ne'er, no ne'er from thy station hadst flown, Her bosom's the man-

MUSICAL MISCELLANY.   101

fion of peace. Thou peace.

SONG XXXVIII.

QUEEN MARY'S FAREWELL TO FRANCE.

O! thou lov'd country, where my youth was  spent, Dear golden days, All paſt in ſweet content, Where the fair morning of my clouded day  Shone mildly bright, and temperately gay. Dear  France, adieu, a long and ſad farewel! No thought  can image, and no tongue can tell, The pangs

I feel at that drear word---farewell!

The ſhip that wafts me from thy friendly ſhore,
   Conveys my body, but conveys no more.
My ſoul is thine, that ſpark of heav'nly flame,
   That better portion of my mingled frame,
Is wholy thine, that part I give to thee,
   That in the temple of thy memory,
The other ever may enſhrined be.

104   THE EDINBURGH

SONG XXXIX.
ONCE MORE I'LL TUNE.

Once more I'll tune the vo-cal shell, To hills and dales my paſ-ſion tell, A flame which time can ne----ver quell, That burns for lovely Peggy. Ye greater bards the lyre ſhould hit, For ſay what ſubject is more fit, Than to re-cord the ſpark-ling wit, and bloom of love-ly Peg-gy?

The fun firſt riſing in the morn,
That paints the dew-beſpangled thorn,
Does not ſo much the day adorn,
   As does my lovely Peggy,
And when in Thetis lap to reſt,
He ſtreaks with gold the ruddy weſt,
He's not ſo beauteous, as undreſs'd
   Appears my lovely Peggy.

Were ſhe array'd in ruſtic weed,
With her the bleating flocks I'd feed,
And pipe upon mine oaten reed,
   To pleaſe my lovely Peggy.
With her a cottage would delight,
All's happy when ſhe's in my ſight,
But when ſhe's gone it's endleſs night,
   All's dark without my Peggy.

The zephyr's air the violet blows,
Or breathe upon the damaſk roſe,
He does not half the ſweets diſcloſe,
   That does my lovely Peggy.
I ſtole a kiſs the other day,

And trust me, nought but truth I say,
The fragrant breath of blooming May,
   Was not so sweet as Peggy.

While bees from flow'r to flow'r shall rove,
And linnets warble thro' the grove,
Or stately swans the waters love,
   So long will I love Peggy.
And when Death with his pointed dart,
Shall strike the blow that rives my heart,
My word shall be when I depart,
   Adieu! my lovely Peggy.

SONG XL.

OSCAR'S GHOST.

O see that form that faintly gleams! 'Tis  Oscar come to cheer my dreams: On wings of  wind he flies away, O stay, my lovely Oscar, stay!

Wake Ossian, last of Fingal's line,
And mix thy tears and sighs with mine.
Awake the Harp to doleful lays,
And soothe my soul with Oscar's praise.
The Shell is ceas'd in Oscar's Hall,
Since gloomy Kerbar wrought the fall:
The Roe on Morven lightly bounds,
Nor hears the cry of Oscar's hounds.

SONG XLI.
BUSK YE, BUSK YE.

Busk ye, busk ye, my bon-ny bride, Busk ye, busk ye, my winsome marrow, Busk ye, busk ye, my bonny bride, And let us to the braes of Yarrow. There will we sport and gather dew, Dancing while lav'rocks sing in the morning. There learn frae turtles to prove true, O Bell ne'er vex me with thy scorning!

To westlin breezes Flora yields,
   And when the beams are kindly warming,
Blythness appears o'er all the fields,
   And nature looks mair fresh and charming.
Learn frae the burns that trace the mead,
   Tho' on their banks the roses blossom,
Yet hastily they flow to Tweed,
   And pour their sweetness in his bosom.

Haste ye, haste ye, my bonny Bell,
   Haste to my arms, and there I'll guard thee.
With free consent my fears repel,
   I'll with my love and care reward thee.
Thus sang I saftly to my fair,
   Wha rais'd my hopes with kind relenting,
O! Queen of Smiles, I ask nae mair,
   Since now my bonny Bell's consenting.

SONG XLII.

THE FAIRY.

A MIDNIGHT MADRIGAL.

Fairest of the virgin train, That trip it o'er the ma-gic plain: Come and dance and sing with me, Under yonder aged tree: Come, and dance and sing with me, under yonder aged tree.

There I'll tell you many a tale,
Of mountain, rock, of hill and dale,
Which will make you laugh with me,
Under yonder aged tree.

See the moon all silver bright,
Shining with a tenfold light,
To try to see my Queen with me,
Thro' the boughs of yonder tree.

Who is that which I espy,
Just descended from thy sky?
E'en faith 'tis Cupid, come to see
My fair beneath yon aged tree.

A little rogue! but he shall smart—
I'll take away his bow and dart,
And give them, 'fore his face, to thee,
Under yonder aged tree.

Then we'll play, and dance, and sing,
Celebrating Pan our king,
And I'll always live with thee,
Under yonder aged tree

SONG XLIII.
ANNA'S URN.

Encompafs'd in an angel's frame, An angel's virtues lay: Too foon did heaven affert its claim, And call'd its own away, and call'd its own away. My Anna's worth, my Anna's charms Can never more return, Can never more return! What then fhall fill thefe widow'd arms? Ah ———— me! Ah me! Ah me! my

An - na's urn!

Can I forget that blifs refin'd,
  Which, bleft with her, I knew?
Our hearts, in facred bonds entwin'd,
  Were bound by love too true.
That rural train, which once were uf'd
  In feftive dance to turn,
So pleaf'd, when Anna they amufed,
  Now weeping deck her Urn.

The foul efcaping from its chain,
  She clafp'd me to her breaft,
" To part with thee is all my pain!"
  She cried! then funk to reft!
While mem'ry fhall her feat retain,
  From beauteous Anna torn,
My heart fhall breathe its ceafelefs ftrain
  Of forrow o'er her Urn.

There with the earlieft dawn, a dove
  Laments her murder'd mate:
There Philomela, loft to love,
  Tells the pale moon her fate.
With yew, and ivy round me fpread,
  My Anna there I'll mourn;
For all my foul, now fhe is dead,
  Concentres in her Urn.

SONG XLIV.

BLUE-EYED PATTY:
OR,
THE ORIGIN OF THE PATTEN.

Sweet ditties would my Patty sing, Old Chevy Chace, God save the king, Fair Rosemy and Sawny Scot, Lil-li-bul-le-ro, and what not: All these would sing my blue-ey'd Pat-ty, As with her pail she trudg'd along: While still the burden of her song, My hammer beat to blue-ey'd Patty,

While still the bur-den of her song, My hammer beat to blue-ey'd Patty, My hammer beat to blue-ey'd Pat-ty, My hammer beat to blue-ey'd Pat--ty.

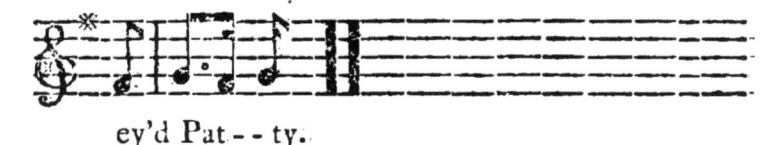

But nipping frosts and chilling rain,
Too soon alas! choak'd every strain,
Too soon alas! the miry way
Her wet shod feet did sore dismay;
   And hoarse was heard my blue ey'd Patty:
While I for very mad did cry,
Ah! cou'd I but again, said I,
   Hear the sweet voice of blue-ey'd Patty.

Love taught me how: I work'd I sung,
My anvil glow'd, my hammer rung,

Till I had form'd, from out the fire,
To bear her feet above the mire,
   An engine for my blue-ey'd Patty.
Again was heard each tuneful close,
My fair one on the *Patten* rose,
   Which takes its name from blue-ey'd *Patty*.

SONG XLV.

FOR FREEDOM AND HIS NATIVE LAND.

Andantino.

Must peace and pleasure's melting strain For e - - - ver in this circle reign? A while the muse with ardour glows, To pay the debt that Britain owes, To pay the debt that Bri - tain

owes. O wave a while your soft delights! To praise each valiant son that fights, And braves abroad each hos-tile band, And braves abroad each hostile band, For freedom, freedom, For freedom and his native land - - - - - - - - For free - dom and his native land, For freedom, freedom, freedom, and his native land.

The foldier feeks a diftant plain,
The failor ploughs the boift'rous main:
Their toil domeftic eafe fecures,
The labour theirs, the pleafure yours:
Then change a while your foft delights,
To praife each valiant fon that fights,
And braves abroad each hoftile band,
For freedom and his native land.

Ye wealthy, who domeftic fweets,
Enjoy within your gay retreats,
Think, think, on thofe who guard the fhore,
While unmolefted fprings your ftore:
And change a while your foft delights,
To praife each valiant fon that fights,
And braves abroad each hoftile band,
For freedom and his native land.

Ye fwains who haunt the fhady grove,
And tranquil breathe your vows of love,
Who hear not war's tremendous voice,
But in the arms of peace rejoice:
Change, change a while your foft delights,
To praife each valiant fon that fights,

And braves abroad each hoftile band,
For freedom and his native land.

And ye, who in this frolic train,
Infpir'd with mufic's fprightly ftrain,
And wild with pleafure's airy round,
Bid flowing bowls with love be crown'd:
Amid your focial dear delights,
Remember him who boldly fights,
And braves abroad each hoftile band,
For freedom and his native land.

SONG XLVI.

THOU ART GONE AWA FROM ME, MARY.

Thou art gone awa, thou art gone awa, thou art gone awa from me, Ma-ry; Nor friends nor I could make thee ſtay, Thou haſt cheated them and me, Ma-ry. Until this hour I ne-ver thought that ought could alter thee, Mary: Thour't ſtill the miſtreſs of my heart, Think what you will of me Ma--ry.

What e'er he said or might pretend,
   That stole that heart of thine, Mary;
True love I'm sure was ne'er his end,
   Or nae such love as mine, Mary.
I spoke sincere nor flatter'd much,
   Had no unworthy thoughts, Mary;
Ambition, wealth, nor naething such,
   No—I lov'd only thee, Mary.

Tho' you've been false, yet while I live,
   No other maid I'll woo, Mary;
Till friends forget, and I forgive
   Thy wrongs to them and me, Mary.
So then farewell: of this be sure,
   Since you've been false to me, Mary;
For all the world I'd not endure,
   Half what I've done for thee, Mary.

SONG XLVII.

THE HEAVY HOURS.

Largo andante.

The heavy hours are almost past That part my love and me; My longing eyes may hope at last their only wish to see. But how, my Delia, will you meet The man you've lost so long? Will love in all your pulses beat, And tremble on your tongue? Will love in all your pulses beat, And tremble on your tongue?

Will you in ev'ry look declare
   Your heart is ſtill the ſame?
And heal each idly anxious care,
   Our fears in abſence frame?
Thus, Delia, thus I paint the ſcene,
   When we ſhall ſhortly meet;
And try what yet remains between,
   Of loit'ring time to cheat!

But if the dream that ſoothes my mind,
   Shall falſe and groundleſs prove;
If I am doom'd at length to find
   You have forgot to love:
All I of Venus aſk is this,
   No more to let us join;
But grant me here the flatt'ring bliſs,
   To die and think you mine.

SONG XLVIII.

THE SUMMER WAS OVER.

The summer was o-ver, my flocks were all shorn, My meadows were mow'd, And I'd hous'd all my corn, Fair Phillida's cottage was just in my view, A-wooing I went I had nought else to do. On Flora's soft sopha together we sat, And spent some long hours in amorous chat. I told her I lov'd, and I hop'd she lov'd too, Then kiss'd *her sweet lips, I had nought else to do, I had nought else to do, Then kiss'd her sweet lips, I had nought else to do.*

She hung down her head and with blushes reply'd,
I'll love you, but first you must make me your bride.
Without hesitation, I make her a vow,
To make her my wife—I had nought else to do.
To the village in quest of a priest did we roam,
By fortune's decree, the grave Don was at home,
I gave him a fee to make one of us two;
He married us then—he had nought else to do.

E'er since we've been happy with peace and content,
Nor tasted the sorrows of those who repent,
Our neighbours all round us we love, and 'tis true,
Each other beside!—when we've nought else to do,
With Phœbus the toil of the day we begin,
I shepherd my flock, while she sits down to spin,
Our cares thus domestic we'll arduous pursue,
And ever will love—when we've nought else to do.

SONG XLIX.
LEADER HAUGHS AND YARROW.

The morn was fair, saft was the air, All Nature's sweets were springing: The buds did bow with silver dew, Ten thousand birds were singing, When on the bent, with blyth content, young Jamie sang his marrow, Nae bonnier lass e'er trode the grass on Leader-haughs and Yarrow.

How sweet her face, where every grace
In heavenly beauty's planted!

Her smiling e'en and comely mein,
  That nae perfection wanted.
I'll never fret, nor ban my fate,
  But bless my bonny marrow:
If her dear smile my doubts beguile,
  My mind shall ken nae sorrow.

Yet tho' she's fair, and has full share
  Of ev'ry charm inchanting,
Each good turns ill, and soon will kill
  Poor me, if love be wanting.
O bonny lass! have but the grace
  To think ere ye gae further,
Your joys maun flit, if you commit
  The crying sin of murder.

My wand'ring ghaist will ne'er get rest,
  And day and night affright ye;
But if ye're kind, and joyful mind,
  I'll study to delight ye.
Our years around with love thus crown'd,
  From all things joy shall borrow:
Thus none shall be more blest than we,
  On leader-haughs and Yarrow.

O sweetest Sue! 'tis only you
  Can make life worth my wishes,
If equal love your mind can move
  To grant this best of blisses.
Thou art my sun, and thy least frown
  Would blast me in the blossom:
But if thou shine, and make me thine,
  I'll flourish in thy bosom.

SONG L.

HOW BLEST THE MAID.

Larghetto.

How bleſt the maid whoſe boſom No headſtrong paſſion knows, Her days in joys ſhe paſ-ſes, Her nights in calm repoſe. Where'er her fan-cy leads her, No pain, no fear invades her, But pleaſure without meaſure from every object flows. No pain, no fear. Where'er ſhe goes, How bleſt the maid whose bosom no headstrong pas-sion knows, Her days in joys she passes, Her nights in calm repose. Where'er her fancy leads, No pain no fear invades, No fear invades, no fear invades.

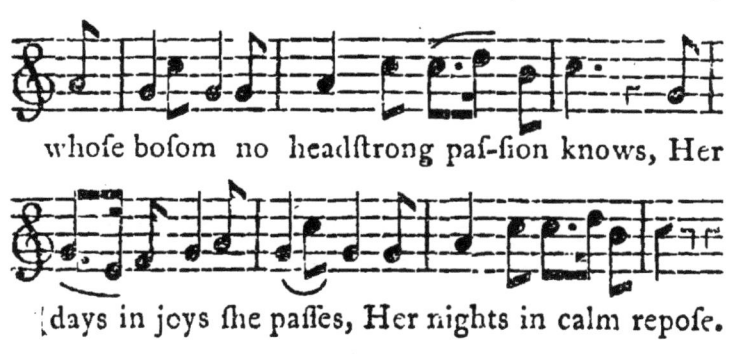

SONG LI.

HAD I A HEART.

Had I a heart for falsehood fram'd, I ne'er could injure you; For tho' your tongue no promise claim'd, your charms would make me true. To you no soul shall bear deceit, No stranger offer wrong; But friends in all the ag'd you'll meet, And lovers in the young.

But when they learn that you have bleft
   Another with your heart,
They'll bid afpiring paffion reft,
   And act a brother's part.
Then, lady, dread not here deceit,
   Nor fear to fuffer wrong,
For friends in all the ag'd you'll meet,
   And brothers in the young.

SONG LII.

GRAMACHREE MOLLY.

TO THE FOREGOING TUNE.

As down on Banna's banks I ftray'd,
   One evening in May,
The little birds, in blytheft notes,
   Made vocal ev'ry fpray:
They fung their little tales of love
   They fung them o'er and o'er;
Ah Gramachree, ma Colleenouge,
   Ma Molly Afhtore!

The daify pied, and all the fweets
   The dawn of nature yields;
The primrofe pale, the vi'let blue,
   Lay fcatter'd o'er the fields:

Such fragrance in the bosom lies
　　Of her whom I adore.
　　　　　　Ah Gramachree, &c.

I laid me down upon a bank,
　　Bewailing my sad fate,
That doom'd me thus the slave of love,
　　And cruel Molly's hate:
How can she break the honest heart
　　That wears her in its core?
　　　　　　Ah Gramachree, &c.

You said you lov'd me, Molly dear!
　　Ah! why did I believe?
Yet, who could think such tender words
　　Were meant but to deceive?
That love was all I ask'd on earth,
　　Nay, heav'n could give no more.
　　　　　　Ah Gramachree, &c.

Oh had I all the flocks that graze
　　On yonder yellow hill,
Or low'd for me the num'rous herds
　　That yon green pasture fill;
With her I love I'd gladly share
　　My kine and fleecy store.
　　　　　　Ah Gramachree, &c.

Two turtle doves above my head
　　Sat courting on a bough;

I envied not their happinefs,
   To fee them bill and coo:
Such fondnefs once for me fhe fhew'd;
   But now, alas! 'tis o'er.
          Ah Gramachree, &c.

Then fare thee well, my Molly dear,
   Thy lofs I e'er fhall mourn;
Whilft life remains in Strephon's heart,
   'Twill beat for thee alone:
Tho' thou art falfe, may heaven on thee
   Its choiceft bleffings pour.
          Ah Gramachree, &c.

SONG LIII.

FOR EVER FORTUNE.

For ever, Fortune, wilt thou prove An unrelenting foe to love? And when we meet a mutual heart, Come in between and bid us part?

Bid us sigh on, from day to day, And wish and wish our souls away, Till youth and genial years are flown, And all the life of life is gone

But busy, busy still art thou
  To bind the loveless, joyless vow;
The heart from pleasure to delude,
  To bind the gentle with the rude.

For once, O Fortune, hear my pray'r,
  And I absolve thy future care;
All other blessings I resign,
  Make but the dear Amanda mine.

SONG LIV.

THE BANKS OF BANNA.

Shepherds, I have lost my love, Have you seen my Anna, Pride of ev'ry shady grove, Upon the banks of Banna. I for her my home forsook Near yon misty mountain, Left my flock, my pipe, my crook, greenwood shade, and fountain.

Never shall I see them more,
   Until her returning;
All the joys of life are o'er,
   From gladness chang'd to mourning:

Whither is my charmer flown,
   Shepherds tell me whither,
Ah! woe for me, perhaps she's gone
   For ever, and for ever.

SONG LV.

PINKY HOUSE.

By Pin--kie houſe oft let me walk,

While cir--cled in my arms, I hear my Nel-

ly ſweetly talk, And gaze o'er all her charms

O let me e-ver fond behold thoſe gra-

ces void of art, Thoſe chearful ſmiles that

ſweet-ly hold in will-ing chains my heart.

O come, my love, and bring anew
   That gentle turn of mind;
That gracefulness of air, in you,
   By nature's hand defign'd:
That beauty like the blufhing rofe,
   Firft lighted up this flame!
Which, like the fun, for ever glows
   Within my breaft the fame.

Ye light coquets! ye airy things!
   How vain is all your art!
How feldom it a lover brings!
   How rarely keeps a heart!
O gather from my Nelly's charms,
   That fweet, that graceful eafe;
That blufhing modefty that warms;
   That native art to pleafe!

Come then, my love, O! come along,
   And feed me with thy charms;
Come, fair infpirer of my fong,
   O fill my longing arms!
A flame like mine can never die,
   While charms, fo bright as thine,
So heav'nly fair, both pleafe the eye,
   And fill the foul divine.

140 THE EDINBURGH

SONG LVI.
JAMIE GAY.

As Ja-mie Gay gaed blithe his way Along the banks of Tweed, A bonny lass as e-ver was came tripping o'er the mead. The hear-ty swain, un-taught to feign, The buxom nymph survey'd, And full of glee, As lad could be, Bespoke the blooming maid.

Dear lassie, tell, why by thysell
  Thou lonely wander'st here?
My ewes, she cry'd, are straying wide;
  Canst tell me, laddie, where?
To town I hie, he made reply,
  Some pleasing sport to see:
But thou'rt so neat, so trim, so sweet,
  I'll seek thy ewes with thee.

She gave her hand, nor made a stand;
  But lik'd the youth's intent:
O'er hill and dale, o'er plain and vale,
  Right merrily they went.
The birds sang sweet, the pair to greet,
  And flow'rets bloom'd around;
And as they walk'd, of love they talk'd,
  And lovers joys when crown'd.

And now the sun had rose to noon,
  The zenith of his pow'r,
When to the shade their steps they made
  To pass the mid-day hour.
The bonny lad row'd in his plaid
  The lass, who scorn'd to frown:
She soon forgot the ewes she sought,
  And he to gang to town.

SONG LVII.

THE BROOM ON COWDENKNOWS.

When summer comes, the swains on Tweed sing their suc-cefs-ful loves; A-round the ewes and lambkins feed, And music fills the groves: But my lov'd song is then the broom so fair on Cowdenknows; For sure so soft so sweet a bloom Elsewhere there ne--ver grows.

Oh the broom, the bonny bonny broom, the
broom on Cowdenknows; For sure so soft, so 
sweet a bloom Elsewhere there ne-ver grows. 

There Colin tun'd his oaten reed,
    And won my yielding heart;
No shepherd e'er that dwelt on Tweed
    Could play with half such art.
He sung of Tay, of Forth, and Clyde
    The hills and dales all round;
Of Leader haughs and Leader side,
    Oh! how I bless'd the found.
        Oh! the broom, &c.

Not Tiviot braes, so green and gay,
    May with its broom compare;
Not Yarrow banks, in flow'ry May,
    Nor the Bush aboon Traquair.

More pleasing far are Cowdenknows,
My peaceful happy home,
Where I was wont to milk my ewes
At eve among the broom.
Oh! the broom, &c.

SONG LVIII.

STILL THE LARK FINDS REPOSE.

Andante.

Still the lark finds re - - pose in the full wa-

ving corn, Or the bee on the rose, tho' sur-

rounded with thorn. Never robb'd of their

ease, they are thoughtless and free: But no

more gentle peace shall e'er harbour with me.

e'er harbour with me. Still the lark finds re-

pose, in the full waving corn, Or the bee on

the rose, tho' surrounded with thorn: Still in

search of delight, every pleasure they prove, Ne'er

torment-ed by pride, nor the flights of fond

love, the flights of fond love, the flights of fond

love. Still the lark finds repose in the full  waving corn, Or the bee on the rose, tho' surrounded with thorn.

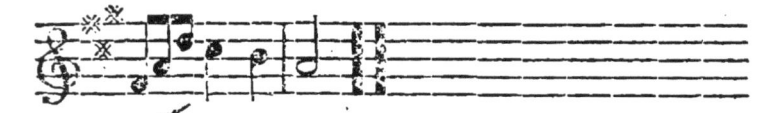

SONG LIX.

MY LODGING IS ON THE COLD GROUND.

My lodging is on the cold ground, And  ve-ry hard is my fare; But that which grieves me more, love, Is the coldness of my dear - -

Yet still he cry'd, turn love, I pray thee, love,

turn to me; For thou art the on - ly girl,

love, that is ado - red by me.

With a garland of straw I'll crown thee, love,
   I'll marry thee with a rush ring;
Thy frozen heart shall melt with love,
   So merrily I shall sing.
      Yet still, &c.

But if you will harden your heart, love,
   And be deaf to my pitiful moan:
Oh! I must endure the smart, love,
   And tumble in straw all alone.
      Yet still, &c.

SONG LX.

THE BANKS OF THE DEE.

'Twas fummer, and foftly the breezes were blowing, And fweetly the nightingale fung from the tree; At the foot of a rock where the river was flowing, I fat myfelf down on the banks of the Dee. Flow on, lovely Dee, flow on thou fweet river, Thy banks, pureft ftream, fhall be dear to me ever: For there I firſt gain'd the affection and favour Of Ja-mie the glory and pride of the Dee.

But now he's gone from me, and left me thus mourn‑
    ing,
To quell the proud rebels---for valiant is he;
And ah! there's no hopes of his ſpeedy returning,
To wander again on the Banks of the Dee.
He's gone, hapleſs youth, o'er the loud-roaring bil‑
    lows,
The kindeſt and ſweeteſt of all the gay fellows,
And left me to ſtray 'mongſt the once loved willows,
The lonlieſt maid on the Banks of the Dee.

  But time and my prayers may perhaps yet reſtore
    him,
Bleſt peace may reſtore my dear ſhepherd to me;
And when he returns, with ſuch care I'll watch
    o'er him,

He never shall leave the sweet Banks of the Dee.
The Dee then shall flow, all its beauties displaying;
The lambs on its banks shall again be seen playing;
While I, with my Jamie, am carelessly straying,
And tasting again all the sweets of the Dee.

ADDITIONS BY A LADY.

Thus sung the fair maid on the banks of the river,
And sweetly re-cho'd each neighbouring tree;
But now all these hopes must evanish for ever,
Since Jamie shall ne'er see the Banks of the Dee.
On a foreign shore the sweet youth lay dying,
In a foreign grave his body's now lying;
While friends and acquaintaince in Scotland are crying
For Jamie the glory and pride of the Dee.

Mis-hap on the hand by whom he was wounded;
Mis-hap on the wars that call'd him away
From a circle of friends by which he was surround-(ed,
Who mourn for dear Jamie the tedious day.
Oh! poor hapless maid, who mourns discontented,
The loss of a lover so justly lamented;
By time, only time, can her grief be contented,
And all her dull hours become chearful and gay.

'Twas honour and brav'ry made him leave her mourning,

From unjuſt rebellion his country to free ;
He left her in hopes of a ſpeedy returning,
To wander again on the Banks of the Dee.
For this he deſpiſed all dangers and perils ;
'Twas thus he eſpouſed Britannia's quarrels,
That when he came home he might crown her with
    laurels,
The happieſt maid on the Banks of the Dee.

  But fate had determin'd his fall to be glorious,
Tho' dreadful the thought muſt be unto me ;
He fell, like brave Wolfe, when the troops were
    victorious ;
Sure each tender heart muſt bewail the decree :
Yet, tho' he is gone, the once faithful lover,
And all our fine ſchemes of true happineſs over,
No doubt he implored his pity and favour
For me he had left on the Banks of the Dee.

SONG LXI.

TAK' YOUR AULD CLOAK ABOUT YE.

In winter when the rain rain'd cauld, And froſt and ſnaw on il - - - ka hill, And Boreas wi' his blaſts ſae bauld, was threat'ning a' our ky to kill; Then Bell my wife, who loe's nae ſtrife, She ſaid to me right haf-ti-ly, Get up, gudeman, ſave Crummy's life, And tak' your auld cloak a - bout ye.

My Crummy is a ufeful cow,
 And fhe is come of a guid kine;
Aft has fhe wet the bairns mou',
 And I am laith that fhe fhould tyne:
Get up, gudeman, it is fu' time,
 The fun fhines in the lift fae hie;
Sloth never made a gracious end,
 Gae tak' your auld cloak about ye.

My cloak was anes a guid gray cloak,
 When it was fitting for my wear;
But now its fcantly worth a groat,
 For I have worn't this thirty year.
Let's fpend the gear that we have won,
 We little ken the day we'll die;
Then I'll be proud, fince I have fworn
 To have a new cloak about me.

In days when our king Robert rang,
 His trews they coft but half a crown;
He faid they were a groat o'er dear,
 And ca'd the taylor thief and lown.
He was the king that wore a crown,
 And thou the man of laigh degree,
'Tis pride puts a' the country down,
 Sae tak' thy auld cloak about ye.

Every land has its ain laugh,
   Ilk kind of corn it has its hool;
I think the warld is a' run wrang,
   When ilka wife her man wad rule.
Do ye not see Rob, Jock, and Hab,
   As they are girded gallantly?
While I sit hurklen in the ase---
   I'll have a new cloak about me.

Gudeman, I wat 'tis thirty years
   Since we did ane anither ken;
And we have had between us twa
   Of lads and bonny lasses ten:
Now they are women grown and men.
   I wish and pray well may they be
And if you prove a good husband,
   E'en tak' your auld cloak about ye.

Bell my wife she lo'es nae strife;
   But she wad guide me if she can:
And, to maintain an easy life,
   I aft maun yield, though I'm gudeman.
Nought's to be won at woman's hand,
   Unless ye give her a' the plea:
Then I'll leave aff where I began,
   And tak' my auld cloak about me.

MUSICAL MISCELLANY. 155

SONG LXII.
CONTENT.

O'er moorlands and mountains, rude, barren, and bare, As wearied and wilder'd I roam, A gentle young shepherdess sees my despair, And leads me o'er lawns to her home. Yellow sheaves from rich Ce-res her cottage had crown'd, Green rushes were strew'd on the floor; Her casement sweet woodbines crept wanton--ly round,

And deckt the sod-seats at the door.

We sat ourselves down to a cooling repast,
  Fresh fruits, and she cull'd me the best;
Whilst thrown from my guard by some glances
    she cast,
  Love slily stole into my breast.
I told my soft wishes, she sweetly reply'd,
  (Ye virgins, her voice was divine!)
" I've rich ones rejected, and great ones deny'd,
  " Yet take me, fond shepherd, I'm thine."

Her air was so modest, her aspect so meek,
  So simple--tho' sweet--were her charms;
I kiss'd the ripe roses that glow'd on her cheek,
  And lock'd the dear maid in my arms.
Now jocund together we tend a few sheep,
  And if on the banks by the stream,
Reclin'd on her bosom, I sink into sleep,
  Her image still softens my dream.

Together we range o'er the flow rifing hills,
  - Delighted with paftoral views;
Or reft on the rock whence the ftreamlet diftils,
  And mark out new themes for my mufe.
To pomp or proud titles fhe ne'er did afpire,
  The damfel's of humble defcent;
The cottager *Peace* is well known for her fire,
  The fhepherds have nam'd her CONTENT.

SONG LXV.

JOHNNY AND MARY.

Down the burn and thro' the mead, His golden locks wav'd o'er his brow, Johnny lilting tun'd his reed, And Mary wip'd her bonny mou'. Dear she lo'ed the well-known song, While her Johnny, blyth and bonny, Sung her praise the whole day long. Down the burn and thro' the mead his gol-den locks wav'd o'er his brow; John-ny lilt-ing tun'd his reed, And Ma-ry wip'd her bon--ny mou'.

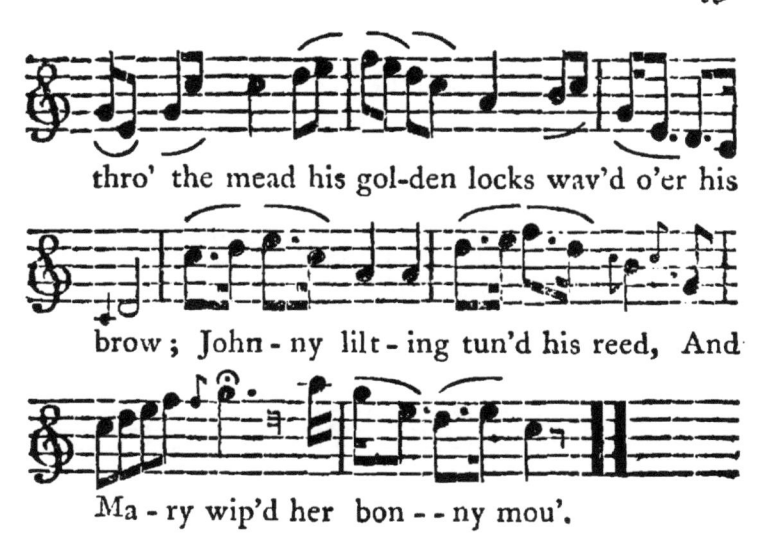

Coſtly claiths ſhe had but few;
Of rings and jewels nae great ſtore;
Her face was fair, her love was true,
And Johnny wiſely wiſh'd nae more:
Love's the pearl the ſhepherds prize;
O'er the mountain---near the fountain,
Love delights the ſhepherd's eyes,
    Down the burn, &c.

Gold and titles give not health,
And Johnny cou'd nae theſe impart;
Youthfu' Mary's greateſt wealth
Was ſtill her faithfu' Johnny's heart:
Sweet the joy's the lovers find,
Great the treaſure,- -ſweet the pleaſure,
Where the heart is always kind.
    Down the burn, &c.

SONG LXVI.

THE ROYAL COTTAGER.

When-e'er I think on that dear spot, On which I fix'd my ru-ral cot; Then while my rose hung on my arm, All free from guile and free from harm, My days they glid-ed on with glee, And all things then were well with me: My days they glided on with glee,

And all things then were well with me.

But when once drawn away by fate
Unto a more exalted ſtate,
By ſmiling Fortune promiſ'd fair
Until ſhe brought her train of care:
'Twas then I firſt began to ſee
That happineſs had fled from me.

The noiſe of cities, glare of courts,
Where gay diſſimulation ſports,
Where envy fain wou'd blight my Roſe,
Becauſe her cheek ſo purely glows;
Let fortune take her ſtores again,
Give me my cot, and rural plain.

And while I tread the ocean's ſide,
The greateſt pleaſure, greateſt pride,
Shall be each day with Roſe to walk,
In ſocial inoffenſive talk;
And when each bliſsful day ſhall cloſe,
The waves ſhall lull us to repoſe.

SONG LXVII.

PEGGY PERKINS.

Let bards elate of Sue and Kate, And Mog-
gy take their fill, O; And pleas'd rehearse in 
jingling verse, The Lass of Richmond hill, O, 
The lass of Richmond hill, O. A lass more 
bright my am'rous flight, Impell'd by Love's fond 
workings, Shall fondly sing, like a-ny thing, 'Tis

charming Peggy Perkins, Peggy Perkins, Peggy Perkins, Peggy Perkins, Peggy Perkins. Shall loudly sing, like a - - ny thing, 'Tis charming Peg-gy Perkins.

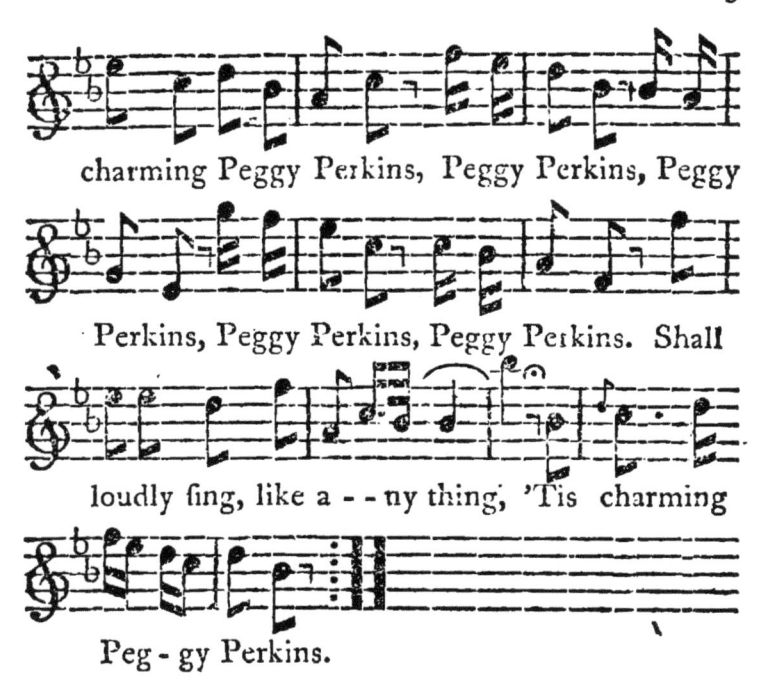

Some men compare the fav'rite fair
  To every thing in nature;
Her eyes divine are funs that shine,
  And so on with each feature.
Leave, leave ye fools, these hackneyed rules,
  And all such subtile quirkings;
Sun, moon, and stars, are all a farce,
  Compar'd to Peggy Perkins.

Each twanging dart that through my heart
  From Cupid's bow has morric'd,
Were it a tree---why I should be
  For all the world a forest!

Five hundred fops, with shrugs and hops,
    And leers, and smiles, and smirkings,
Most willing she would leave for me—
    Oh what a Peggy Perkins!

SONG LXVIII.

THE BLATHRIE O'T.

When I think on this warld's pelf, And the little wi' share I ha'e o't to myself, And how the lass that wants it is by the lads forgot, May the shame fa' the gear and the bla-thrie o't.

Jockie was the laddie that held the pleugh,
But now he's got gowd and gear eneugh;
He thinks nae mair of me that wears the plaiden coat;
        May the shame, &c.

Jenny was the lassie that mucked the byre,
But now she is clad in her silken attire,
And Jockie says he loes her, and swears he's me forgot;
        May the shame, &c.

But all this shall never danton me,
Sae lang as I keep my fancy free:
For the lad that's sae inconstant, he is not worth a groat;
        May the shame, &c.

SONG LXIX.

JENNY MAY.

When Phœbus first salutes the east, And  dew-drops deck each thorn, When ploughmen  shake off downy rest, And hunters wind the horn:  Then light as air I seek the shade Where glides  the silver Tay, And tune my pipe to that sweet  maid Whose name is JENNY MAY.

At noon, when fultry fol is found
   To fcorch the verdant plain;
When nimbling flocks are panting round,
   And feem to live in pain;
Then, fhelter'd in the ftraw thatch'd cot,
   I pafs the time away;
The higheft folks I envy not,
   Give me but Jenny May.

When, riding down the diftant weft,
   The god of light declines,
By many varied ftreaks confeft,
   Delightfully he fhines:
With nymphs and fhepherds on the plain,
   I ftill am blithe and gay;
But yet my fofteft, fweeteft ftrain
   Muft flow to Jenny May.

In fpring, in fummer, autumn too,
   In winter's furieft rage,
Days, hours, and months I'll ftill purfue
   My fancy to engage:
For ev'ry moment, ev'ry hour,
   And ev'ry paffing day
Shall, while kind nature gives me pow'r,
   Be true to Jenny May.

SONG LXX.

IN AIRY DREAMS.

Affetuoso.

In airy dreams soft fancy flies My absent love to see, And with the early dawn I rise, Dear youth to think on thee. How swiftly flew the rosy hours, While love and hope were new; Sweet as the breath of op'ning flow'rs, But ah - - - as transient too.

The moments now move slowly on,
    Until thy wish'd return;
I count them oft, as all alone
    The pensive shades I mourn.
Return, return my love, and charm
    Each anxious care to rest;
Thy smiles shall every care disarm,
    And soothe my soul to rest.

SONG LXXI.

THE EGYPTIAN LOVE-SONG.

FROM POTIPHAR'S WIFE TO YOUNG JOSEPH.

Tranſlated from an Oriental Eſſay on Chaſtity.

Sweet doth bluſh the ro-ſy morn-ing, Sweet  doth beam the gliſt'ning dew; Sweeter ſtill the  day a--dorn-ing, Thy dear ſmiles tranſport  my view. Midſt the bloſſoms, fragrance  flow--ing, Why delights the hon--ied bee,

MUSICAL MISCELLANY. 171

sweeter breaths thy-self be-stow-ing? One

kind kiss on me! on me! One kind kiss

on me.

SONG LXXII.

ALLEN BROOKE OF WYNDERMEER.

Say, have you in the village seen, A lovely youth of pen - - five mien? If such a one hath paſſed by, with me-lan-cho-ly in his eye, Where is he gone? Ah! tell me where?—'Tis Allen Brooke of Wyn-der-meer: Where is he gone? Ah! tell me where?

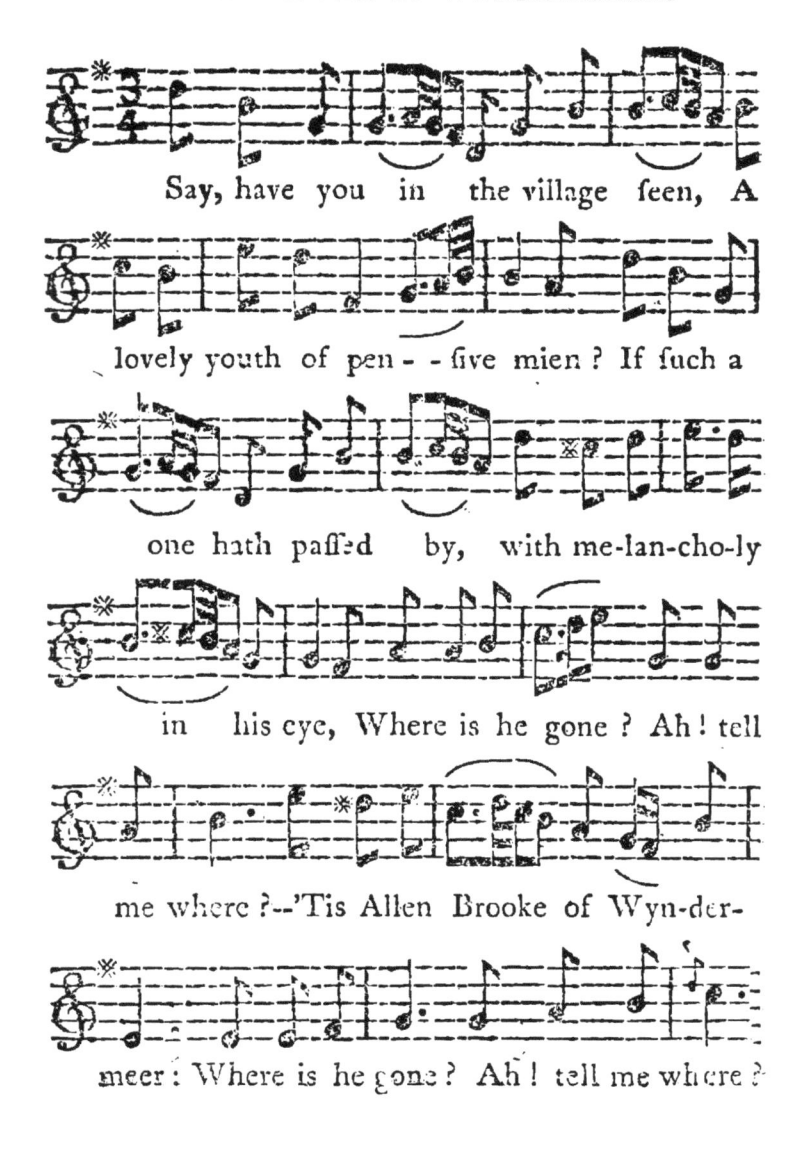

'Tis Allen Brooke ----- of Wyndermeer.

Laſt night he ſighing took his leave,
Which caus'd me all the night to grieve;
And many maids I know there be,
Who try to wean his love from me.
But Heaven knows my heart's ſincere
To Allen Brooke of Wyndermeer.

My throbbing heart is full of woe,
To think that he ſhould leave me ſo:
But if my love ſhould anger'd be,
And try to hide himſelf from me,
Then Death ſhall bear me on a bier
To Allen Brooke of Wyndermeer.

SONG LXXIII.

SWEET ANNIE.

Sweet Annie frae the sea-beach came, Where Jockey speel'd the vessel's side, Ah! wha can keep their heart at hame, When Jockey's tost aboon the tide. Far aff to distant realms he gangs, Yet I'll prove true as he has been; And when ilk lass about him thrangs, He'll think on Annie, his faithful ane.

I met our wealthy laird yeſtreen,
　Wi' gou'd in hand he tempted me,
He praiſ'd my brow, my rolling een,
　And made a brag of what he'd gi'e.
What tho' my Jockey's far away,
　Toſt up and down the onſome main,
I'll keep my heart anither day,
　Since Jockey may return again.

Nae mair, falſe Jamie, ſing nae mair,
　And fairly caſt your pipe away;
My Jocky wad be troubled fair,
　To ſee his friend his love betray:
For a' your ſongs and verſe are vain,
　While Jockey's notes do faithful flow;
My heart to him ſhall true remain,
　I'll keep it for my conſtant jo.

Blaw ſaft, ye gales, round Jocky's head,
　And gar your waves be calm and ſtill;
His hameward ſail with breezes ſpeed,
　And dinna a' my pleaſure ſpill.

What tho' my Jockey's far away,
   Yet he will braw in filler fhine;
I'll keep my heart anither day,
   Since Jockey may again be mine.

SONG LIV.

DONNEL AND FLORA.

When mer-ry hearts were gay, Carelefs of ought but play, Poor Flo-ra flipt away, Sadning to Mora: Loofe flow'd her coal-black hair, quick heav'd her bofom bare, And thus to the troubled air She vented her forrow.

" Loud howls the northern blaſt,
" Bleak is the dreary waſte ;—
" Haſte then, O Donnel haſte,
 " Haſte to thy Flora.
" Twice twelve long months are o'er,
" Since in a foreign ſhore
" You promiſ'd to fight no more,
 " But meet me in Mora.

." Where now is Donnel dear?"
" Maids cry with taunting ſneer,
" Say, is he ſtill ſincere
 " To his lov'd Flora?"
" Parents upbraid by moan,
" Each heart is turn'd to ſtone—
" Ah Flora! thou'rt now alone,
 " Friendleſs in Mora!

" Come, then, O come away,
" Donnel no longer ſtay;
" Where can my rover ſtray
 " From his dear Flora.
" Ah ſure he ne'er could be
" Falſe to his vows to me---
" O heaven! is not yonder he
 " Bounding in Mora?

" Never, O wretched fair,
(Sigh'd the ſad meſſenger)
" Never ſhall Donnel mair
 " Meet his lov'd Flora.

" Cold, cold beyond the main
" Donnel thy love lies slain ;
" He sent me to soothe thy pain
　" Weeping in Mora.

" Well fought our gallant men,
" Headed by brave Burgoyne ;
" Our heroes were thrice led on
　" To British glory,
" But ah! tho' our foes did flee,
" Sad was the loss to thee,
" While every fresh victory
　" Drown'd us in sorrow."

" Here, take this trusty blade,"
(Donnel expiring, said)
" Give it to yon dear maid
　" Weeping in Mora.
" Tell her, O Allan, tell,
" Donnel thus bravely fell,
" And that in his last farewell,
　" He thought on his Flora."

Mute stood the trembling fair,
Speechless with wild despair,
Then striking her bosom bare,
　Sigh'd out poor Flora!
" Oh Donnel! O welladay!"
Was all the fond heart could say ;
At length the sound died away,
　Feebly in Mora.

SONG LXXV.

WILLY WAS A WANTON WAG.

Willy was a wanton wag, The blytheſt lad  that e'er I ſaw, At bridals ſtill he bore the brag  And carried ay the gree awa'. His doublet was  of Zetland ſhag, And vow but Willy he was braw;  At his ſhoulder hang a tag, That pleas'd the

2d Verſe.

laſſes beſt of a'. He was a man

He was a man without a clag,
   His heart was frank without a flaw;
And ay whatever Willy faid,
   It was ftill hadden as a law.
His boots they were made of the jag,
   When he went to the weapon-fhaw
Upon the green nane durft him brag,
   The fiend a ane amang them a'.

And was not Willy well worth gowd,
   He wan the love of great and fma';
For after he the bride had kifs'd,
   He kifs'd the laffes hale-fale a'?
Sae merrily round the ring they row'd,
   When by the hand he led them a',
And fmack on fmack on them beftow'd,
   By virtue of a ftanding law.

And was na Willy a great lown,
   As fhyre a lick as e'er was feen?
When he danc'd with the laffes round,
   The bridegroom fpeer'd where he had been:
Quoth Willy, I've been at the ring,
   With bobbing, faith, my fhanks are fair.
Gae ca' your bride and maidens in,
   For Willy he dow do na mair

Then reft ye, Willy, I'll gae out,
   And for a wee fill up the ring;

But shame light on his souple snout,
    He wanted Willy's wanton fling :
Then straight he to the bride did fare,
    Says, well's me on your bonny face;
With bobbing, Willy's shanks are fair,
    And I'm come out to fill his place.

Bridgroom, she says, you'll spoil the dance,
    And at the ring you'll ay be lag,
Unless, like Willy, ye advance;
    (O ! Willy has a wanton wag :)
For wi't he learns us a to steer,
    And foremost ay bears up the ring;
We will find nae sick dancing here,
    If we want Willy's wanton fling.

SONG LXXVI.

WHEN MORN HER SWEETS.

When morn her fweets fhall firft unfold, And paint the flee-cy clouds with gold, On tuft-ed green O let me play, And welcome up the jo-cund day. Wak'd by the gen-tle voice of love, A--rife, my fair, a--rife and prove The dear delights fond lovers know, The beft of bleffings here below, The beft of bleſſings here below.

To fome clear river's verdant fide,
Do thou my happy footfteps guide;
In concert with the purling ftream
We'll fing, and love fhall be the theme:
E'er night affumes her gloomy reign,
When fhadows lengthen o'er the plain;
We'll to the myrtle grove repair,
For peace and pleafure wait us there.

The laughing god there keeps his court,
And little loves inceffant fport;
Around the winning graces wait,
And calm contentment guards the feat.
There loft in extafies of joy,
While tendereft fcenes our thoughts employ,
We'll blefs the hour our loves begun,
The happy moment made us one.

SONG LXXVII.
FAIR ELIZA.

At Beau-ty's fhrine I long have bow'd, At each new face my heart has glow'd With fomething like a paffion. But dull in-fi-pid joys I found, The blifs no genuine rap-tures crown'd, The fair love but from fa---fhion, The fair love but from fafhion.

Inconstant I of course became,
No care kept up the lambent flame,
   Which thus unheeded died:
To whim was sacrificed each grace,
To vanity each pleasing face,
   And love too oft to pride.

At length I fair Eliza saw,
Whose beauties fire---whose virtues awe;
   I gaz'd, admir'd, and lov'd.
Her sweet attention soothes each care,
Nought can our mutual bliss impair,
   Time has our flame improv'd.

SONG LXXVIII.

THE FLOWING CAN.

A sailor's life's a life of woe, He works now late now early; Now up and down, now to and fro, What then? he takes it cheerly. Bleſt with a ſmiling can of grog, If duty call, ſtand, riſe, or fall, To fates laſt verge he'll jog. The cadge to weigh, the ſheets belay, He does

it with a wish, To heave the lead, or to cat-
head the pond'rous anchor fish: For while the
grog goes round, All sense of danger's drown'd,
We despise it to a man. We sing a little, and
laugh a little, And work a little, And swear a
little: We sing a little, And laugh a little, And
work a little, And swear a little: And fiddle a
little, And foot it a little, And swig the flowing

can, And fiddle a little, And foot it a little,

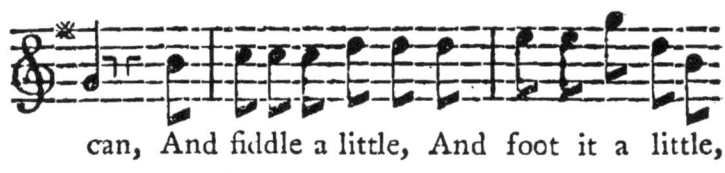

And fwig the flowing can, And fwig the flow-

ing can, And fwig the flowing can.

If howling winds and roaring feas
    Give proof of coming danger,
We view the ftorm, our hearts at eafe,
    For Jack's to fear a ftranger.
Bleft with the fmiling grog, we fly
        Where now below
        We headlong go,
Now rife on mountains high:
        Spight of the gale,
        We hand the fail,
Or take the needful reef;
        Or man the deck,
        To clear fome wreck,
To give the fhip relief.
Though perils threat around,
All fenfe of danger's drown'd,

We defpife it to a man.
  We fing a little, &c.

But yet think not our cafe is hard,
 Though ftorms at fea thus treat us,
For coming home--a fweet reward,
 With fmiles our fweathearts greet us.
Now too the friendly grog we quaff,
  Our am'rous toaft,
  Her we love moft,
And gayly fing and laugh,
  The fails we furl,
  Then for each girl,
The petticoat difplay.
  The deck we clear,
  Then three times cheer,
As we their charms furvey.
And then the grog goes round,
All fenfe of danger's drown'd,
We defpife it to a man.
  We fing a little, &c.

SONG LXXIX.
BILL BOBSTAY.

Tight lads have I fail'd with, but none e'er  so sightly, As honest Bill Bobstay, so kind and  so true: He'd sing like a mermaid, and foot  it so lightly, The forecastle's pride, the delight  of the crew: But poor as a beggar, and often in tat - - ters He went, tho' his fortune was kind without end. For money, cried Bill, and them there fort of mat--ters, For money, cried Bill, and them there fort of matters, What's the good on't d'ye fee, but to fuccour a friend?

There's Nipcheefe, the purfer, by grinding and
 fqueezing,
Firft plund'ring, then leaving the fhip like a rat;
The eddy of fortune ftands on a ftiff breeze in,
And mounts, fierce as fire, a dog-vane in his hat.

My bark, though hard ftorms on life's ocean fhould
 rock her,
Tho' fhe roll in misfortune, and pitch end for end,
No, never fhall Bill keep a fhot in the locker,
 When by handing it out he can fuccour a friend.

Let them throw out their wipes, and cry, fpight of
    the croffes,
And forgetful of toil that fo hard'ly they bore,
That " Sailors at fea earn their money like horfes,
" To fquander it idly like affes afhore."

Such lubbers their a w would coil up, could they
    meafure.
By their feeling, the gen'rous delight without end,
That gives birth in us tars to that trueft of pleafure,
The handing our rhino to fuccour a friend.

Why, what's all this nonfenfe they talks of and pother
All about *rights of men*, what a plague are they at?
If they means that each man to his meffmate's
    a brother,
Why, the lubberly fwabs! ev'ry fool can tell that.

The rights of us Britons we knows to be loyal,
In our country's defence our laft moments to fpend:
To fight up to the ears to protect the blood royal,
To be true to our wives—and to fuccour a friend.

SONG LXXX.

LEAP YEAR.

Won't you hail the leap year, by that am'rous  rogue Janus, Once in ev'ry four times confecrated to Venus? Oh the fine lovely feafon for  frolic and fporting, When the men are made love  to, and girls go a-courting: Then come round  me dear creatures, and frolic and frifk it, And dance it and whisk it, and dance it and whisk it:

Sing smalliow, ba-theshin, ah arrow pat: (*To

be sure dere wont be some fine fun going for-

ward) Faith and conscience and you may say

dat.

Mister Vanus come put on a masculine air,
Throw yourself on your knees, curse your stars, lie
    and swear;
Perfection, says you, to your beauty's a quiz,
Cries Miss Mars, do you love me, I do, dam'me, whiz!
    Then come round me, &c.
(To be sure dere won't be fine sighing and dying and
    wooing and cooing!)
Fait and conscience and you may say dat.

   * To be sung *ad libitum.*

Rich young ladies of fixty new born to love's joys,
Shall hobble and mumble their courtfhip to boys;
Girls fhall court from the fhiners of old men
affiftance,
With their eye on a handfome tight lad in the dif-
tance,
>   Then come round me, &c.

(To be fure they won't make the beft ufe of their
time!)
Fait and confcience and you may fay dat.

Mifs Maypole fhall ftoop to the arms of an imp,
And the tall lady Gauky fhall court my Lord Shrimp,
Mifs Pigmy fhall climb round the neck of a tall man,
And the rich widow Mite court a big Irifh' Jollman!
>   Then come round me, &c.

(To be fure dere won't be fine fimpering and ogling
and leering!)
Fait and confcience and you may fay dat.

Mifs Champanfy, whofe monky has fo many charms,
Of a fine powder'd coxcomb fhall rufh to the arms;
To court Mifter Sciatic Mifs Spafm fhall hop,
And Mifs Cheveux de frize fhall addrefs Mr Crop!
>   Then come round me, &c.

(To be fure de bold little devils won't put the men
in a fine flufteration!)
Fait and confcience and you may fay dat;

Thus you've nothing to do Jollmen all but fit ftill,
And fait ev'ry Jack will foon find out a Jill;

Come on, ye bold devils, swear, lie, and make
 speeches,
'Tis leap-year, and the petticoats govern the breeches!
 Then come round me, &c.
(Ah the dear creatures! to be sure they wont cut a
 comical figure when they are dress'd in their in-
 expressibles!)
Fait and conscience and you may say dat.

SONG LXXXI.

THE LUCKY ESCAPE.

I that once was a ploughman, a sailor am

now. No lark that aloft in the sky, E-ver flut-

ter'd his wings to give speed to the plough Was

so gay and so careless as I, Was so gay and

so careless as I; But my friend was a car-

findo a-board a king's ship, And he ax'd me to

go just to sea for a trip; And he talk'd of such

things as if sailors were kings, And so teazing did

keep, and so teazing did keep, That I left my poor

plough to go ploughing the deep. No long-er the

horn call'd me up in the morn, No longer the

horn call'd me up in the morn, I trusted the carsindo and the inconstant wind, That made me for to go and leave my dear be-hind.

I did not much like for to be aboard a ship,
    When in danger there is no door to creep out;
I liked the jolly tars, I liked bumbo and flip,
    But I did not like rocking about;

By and by came a hurricane, I did not like that,
Next a battle that many a sailor laid flat;
    Ah! cried I, who would roam,
    That like me had a home;
    When I'd sow and I'd reap,
Ere I left my poor plough, to go ploughing the deep,
    Where sweetly the horn
    Call'd me up in the morn,
Ere I trusted the Carsindo and the inconstant wind,
That made me for to go and leave my dear behind.

At laſt ſafe I landed, and in a whole ſkin,
   Nor did I make any long ſtay,
Ere I found by a friend who I ax'd for my kin,
   Father dead, and my wife ran away!
Ah who but thyſelf, ſaid I, haſt thou to blame?
Wives looſing their huſbands oft loſe their good name.
     Ah why did I roam
     When ſo happy at home:
     I could ſow and could reap,
Ere I left my poor plough to go ploughing the deep:
     When ſo ſweetly the horn
     Call'd me up in the morn,
Curſe light upon the Carſindo and inconſtant wind,
That made me for to go and leave my dear behind.

Why if that be the caſe, ſaid this very ſame friend,
   And you ben't no more minded to roam,
Gi'e's a ſhake by the fiſt, all your care's at an end,
   Dad's alive and your wife's ſafe at home.
Stark ſtaring with joy, I leapt out of my ſkin,
Buſſ'd my wife, mother, ſiſter, and all of my kin:
     Now, cried I, let them roam,
     Who want a good home,
     I am well, ſo I'll keep,
Nor again leave my plough to go ploughing the
   deep;
     Once more ſhall the horn
     Call me up in the morn,
Nor ſhall any damn'd Carſindo, nor the inconſtant
   wind
E'er tempt me for to go and leave my dear behind.

SONG LXXXII.

WHEN CUPID HOLDS THE MYRTLE CROWN.

When Cupid holds the myr-tle crown, I'll not the gift de-ny, But gladly feize the pro-fer'd boon Which now compleats my joy, which now compleats my joy. Yet not am-bi-tion prompts me on To rule the wide Defmene, I'd reign a king in love alone That thou might be my queen, I'd reign a king in love alone That thou might be my queen.

Or should the goddess, bright and fair,
  Stoop from the Paphian isle,
And strewing rosy chaplets here,
  On thee prefer to smile:

I'll ne'er repine at this decree,
  Nor other blessing crave;
Sole monarch thou in love shalt be,
  And I thy captive slave.

SONG LXXXIII.

HOW STANDS THE GLASS AROUND.

How ſtands the glaſs around? For ſhame ye take no care, my boys, How ſtands the glaſs a-round? Let mirth and wine a-bound. The trumpets ſound, the colours they are flying, boys, To fight, kill, or wound, May we ſtill be found Content with our hard fate, my boys, On the cold ground.

Why, soldiers, why,
Should we be melancholy, boys?
　　Why, soldiers, why?
　　Whose business 'tis to die!
　　What, sighing? fie!
Don't fear, drink on, be jolly, boys!
　　'Tis he, you, or I!
　　Cold, hot, wet, or dry,
We're always bound to follow, boys,
　　And scorn to fly!

　　'Tis but in vain,—
I mean not to upbraid you, boys,—
　　'Tis but in vain,
　　For soldiers to complain:
　　Should next campaign
Send us to him who made us, boys,
　　We're free from pain!
　　But if we remain,
A bottle and a kind landlady
　　Cure all again.

SONG LXXXIV.

DUMBARTON'S DRUMS.

Dumbarton's drums beat bon-ny O, When they mind me of my dear Johnny O, How happy am I when my foldier is by, While he kiffes and bleffes his Annie O. 'Tis a foldier alone can delight me O For his graceful looks do invite me O: Whilft guarded in his arms, I'll

fear no war's alarms, Neither danger nor death
ſhall e'er fright me, O.

  My love is a handſome laddie, O,
Genteel, but ne'er foppiſh nor gaudy, O;
  Tho' commiſſions are dear,
  Yet I'll buy him one this year,
For he ſhall ſerve no longer a cadie, O.
A ſoldier has honour and bravery, O,
Unacquainted with rogues and their knavery, O!
  He minds no other thing,
  But the ladies or the King;
For every other care is but ſlavery O.

  Then I'll be the Captain's lady, O,
Farewell all my friends and my daddy, O;
  I'll wait no more at home,
  But I'll follow with the drum,
And whene'er that beats, I'll be ready, O.
Dumbarton's Drums ſound bonny, O;
They are ſprightly, like my dear Johnny, O,
  How happy ſhall I be,
  When on my ſoldier's knee,
And he kiſſes and bleſſes his Annie, O.
  Vol. II.   R

SONG LXXXV.

THE OLD MAN'S SONG.

To the foregoing Tune.

O why should old age so much wound us, O?
There is nothing in't at all to confound us, O;
    For how happy now am I,
    With my old wife sitting by,
And our bairns and our oyes all around us, O.
    For how happy now am I, &c.

We began in this world with naething, O,
And we've jogg'd on and toil'd for the aething, O;
    We made use of what we had,
    And our thankful hearts were glad,
When we got the bit meat and the claithing, O.
    We made use of what we had, &c.

When we had any thing we never vaunted, O,
Nor did we hing our heads when we wanted, O;
    We always gave a share
    Of the little we could spare,
When it pleas'd the ALMIGHTY to grant it, O.
    We always gave a share, &c.

We have liv'd all our lifetime contented, O,
Since the day we became first acquainted, O:

It's true we have been poor,
  And we are so to this hour,
Yet we never repin'd nor lamented, O.
  It's true we have been poor, &c.

We never laid a plot to be wealthy, O,
By ways that were cunning or stealthy, O,
  But we always had the bliss,
  (And what further could we wis'?)
To be pleas'd with ourselves and be healthy, O.
  But we always had the bliss, &c.

But tho' we cannot boast of our *guineas*, O,
We have plenty of *Jockies* and *Jeannies*, O;
  And these I'm certain are
  More desireable by far
Than a bag full of poor *yellow stanies*, O.
  And these I'm certain are, &c.

We have seen many wonder and fairly, O,
At changes that have almost been yearly, O,
  Of rich folks up and down,
  Both in country and in town,
That now live but scrimply and sparely, O.
  Of rich folks up and down, &c.

Then why should people brag of prosperity, O,
Since a straiten'd life we see is no rarity, O?
  Indeed we've been in want,
  And our living's been but scant,

Yet we never were reduc'd to feek charity, O.
    Indeed we've been in want, &c.

In this houfe we firft came together, O,
Where we've long been a father and mother, O,
    And tho' not of ftone and lime,
    It will ferve us all our time,
And I hope we fhall never need another, O.
    And tho' not of ftone and lime, &c.

And when we leave this habitation, O
We'll depart with a good commendation, O,
    We'll go hand in hand I wis'
    To a better place than this,
And make room for the next generation, O,
    We'll go hand in hand I wis', &c.

Then why fhould old age fo much wound us, O?
There is nothing in't at all to confound us, O,
    For how happy now am I,
    With my old wife fitting by,
And our bairns and our oyes all around us, O.
    For how happy now am I, &.

SONG LXXXVI.

THERE WAS A JOLLY MILLER.

'There was a jolly miller once Liv'd on the river Dee, He danc'd and he sung from morn till night, No lark so blithe as he. And this the burden of his song for e-ver us'd to be: I care for nobody, no, not I, If no-bo-dy cares for me.

I live by my mill, God bless her! she's kindred,
   child and wife;
I would not change my station for any other in life.
No lawyer, surgeon, or doctor, e'er had a groat from
   me.
I care for nobody, no, not I, if nobody cares for me.

When spring begins its merry career, oh! how his
   heart grows gay!
No summer's drouth alarms his fears, nor winter's
   sad decay;
No foresight mars the miller's joy, who's wont to
   sing and say,
Let others toil from year to year, I live from day to
   day.

Thus, like the miller, bold and free, let us rejoice
   and sing:
The days of youth are made for glee, and time is on
   the wing.
This song shall pass from me to thee, along this
   jovial ring:
Let heart and voice and all agree, to say,—long live
   the King!

SONG LXXXVII.

BRITISH GRENADIERS.

Some talk of Alexander, and some of Her-cu--les, Of Conon and Lysander, and some Mil-ti-a-des; But of all the world's brave heroes there's none that can compare With a tow, row, row, row, row, to the British grenadiers. But of all the world's brave heroes there's none that can compare with a tow, row, row, row, row,

to the Britiſh gre-na-diers.

None of thoſe ancient heroes e'er ſaw a cannon ball,
Or knew the force of powder to ſlay their foes withal;
But our brave boys do know it, and baniſh all their fears,
With a tow, row, row, row, row, the Britiſh Grenadiers.
    But our brave boys, &c

Whene'er we are commanded to ſtorm the Paliſades,
Our leaders march with fuſees, and we with hand Granades,
We throw them from the glacis about our enemies ears,
With a tow, row, row, row, row, the Britiſh Grenadiers,
    We throw them, &c.

The god of war was pleaſed, and great Bellona ſmiles,
To ſee theſe noble heroes of our Britiſh Iſles;

And all the gods celeſtial, deſcended from their
       ſpheres,
Beheld with admiration the Britiſh Grenadiers.
    And all the gods celeſtial, &c.

Then let us crown a bumper, and drink a health to
       thoſe
Who carry caps and pouches that wear the looped
       clothes.
May they and their commanders live happy all their
       years,
With a tow, row, row, row, row, the Britiſh Gre-
       nadiers.
    May they and their commanders, &c.

SONG LXXXVIII.

THE ECHOING HORN.

The echoing horn calls the fportfmen abroad

To horfe, my brave boys, and away. The morn-

ing is up, and the cry of the hounds Upbraids

our too tedious delay. What pleafure we feel in

purfuing the fox! O'er hill and o'er valley he

flies: Then follow, we'll foon overtake him: huzza! The traitor is feiz'd on and dies. He dies - -

- - - - - - - - - - - - - - - The traitor is feiz'd on

Chorus.

and dies. Then follow, we'll foon overtake him,

huzza! The traitor is feiz'd on, and dies.

Triumphant returning at night with the fpoil,
    Like Bacchanals, fhouting and gay;
How fweet with a bottle and lafs to refrefh,
    And drown the fatigues of the day!
With fport, love, and wine, fickle fortune defy;
    Dull wifdom all happinefs fours.
Since life is no more than a paffage at beft,
    Let's ftrew the way over with flow'rs.
    With flow'rs; lets ftrew, &c.

SONG LXXXIX.

HE STOLE MY TENDER HEART AWAY.

The fields were green, the hills were gay, And  birds were finging on each fpray, When Colin  met me in the grove, And told me tender  tales of love. Was ever fwain fo blithe as he?  So kind, fo faithful, and fo free? In fpite of  all my friends could fay, Young Colin ftole my heart away. In spite of all my friends could

say, Young Colin stole my heart away.

Whene'er he trips the meads along,
He sweetly joins the woodlark's song;
And when he dances on the green,
There's none so blithe as Colin seen.
If he's but by I nothing fear;
For I alone am all his care:
Then, spite of all my friends can say,
He's stole my tender heart away.

My mother chides whene'er I roam,
And seems surpris'd I quit my home:
But she'd not wonder that I rove,
Did she but feel how much I love.
Full well I know the gen'rous swain
Will never give my bosom pain:
Then, spite of all my friends can say,
He's stole my tender heart away.

SONG XC.

ONE BOTTLE MORE.

Affift me, ye lads, who have hearts void of guile, To fing in the praifes of old Ireland's ifle. Where true ho-fpi-ta-li-ty o - - pens the door, And friendfhip detains us for one bottle more, one bot-tle more, ar-ra, one bot-tle more, And friendfhip detains us for one bottle more.

Old England, your taunts on our country forbear;
With our bulls, and our brogues, we are true and sincere,
For if but one bottle remain'd in our store,
We have generous hearts to give that bottle more.

In Candy's, in Church-street, I'll sing of a set
Of six Irish blades who together had met;
Four bottles a-piece made us call for our score,
And nothing remained but one bottle more.

Our bill being paid, we were loath to depart,
For friendship had grappled each man by the heart;
Where the least touch you know makes an Irishman roar,
And the whack from shilella brought six bottles more.

Slow Phœbus had shone thro' our window so bright,
Quite happy to view his blest children of light.
So we parted with hearts neither sorry nor sore,
Resolving next night to drink twelve bottles more.

SONG XCI.

BONNY CHRISTY.

How sweetly smells the simmer green! Sweet tastes the peach and cherry: Painting and or-der please our een, And claret makes us mer-ry: But fin-est colours, fruits, and flowers, and wine, tho' I be thir-sty, Lose a' their charms and weak-er powers, Compar'd with those of Chris-ty.

When wand'ring o'er the flow'ry park,
    No natural beauty wanting,
How lightfome is't to hear the lark,
    And birds in concert chanting!
But if my Chrifty tunes her voice,
    I'm rapt in admiration;
My thoughts with ecftafies rejoice,
    And drap the haill creation.

Whene'er fhe fmiles a kindly glance,
    I take the happy omen,
And aften mint to make advance,
    Hoping fhe'll prove a woman:
But dubious of my ain defert,
    My fentiments I fmother;
With fecret fighs I vex my heart,
    For fear fhe loves another.

Thus fang blate Edie by a burn,
    His Chrifty did o'er-hear him;
She doughtna let her lover mourn,
    But e'er he wift drew near him.
She fpake her favour with a look,
    Which left nae room to doubt her:
He wifely this white minute took,
    And flang his arms about her.

My Chrifty!——witnefs, bonny ftream,
    Sic joy frae tears arifing,

I wifh this mayna be a dream;
O love the maift furprifing!
Time was too precious now for talk;
This point of a' his wifhes
He wadna with fet fpeeches bauk,
But war'd it a' on kiffes.

SONG XCII.

FROM THE EAST BREAKS THE MORN.

From the eaft breaks the morn, See the fun-
beams a-dorn The wild heath and the mountains
fo high --, The wild heath and the mountains fo high ----. Shrilly opes the ftaunch hound,

The steed neighs to the sound, And the floods  and the vallies re - - - - - - ply. And the floods  and the val - lies re - - ply.

  Our forefathers, so good,
  Prov'd their greatness of blood
By encount'ring the pard and the boar;
  Ruddy health bloom'd the face,
  Age and youth urg'd the chace,
And taught woodlands and forests to roar.

  Hence of noble descent,
  Hills and wilds we frequent,
Where the bosom of nature's reveal'd;
  'Tho' in life's busy day
  Man of man make a prey,
Still let ours be the prey of the field.

  With the chace in full sight,
  Gods! how great the delight!
How our mutual sensations refine!

Where is care? Where is fear?
Like the winds in the rear,
And the man's loſt in ſomething divine.

Now to horſe, my brave boys;
Lo! each pants for the joys
That anon ſhall enliven the whole :
Then at eve we'll diſmount,
Toils and pleaſures recount,
And renew the chace over the bowl.

SONG XCIII.

LET GAY ONES AND GREAT.

To the foregoing tune.

LET gay ones and great
Make the moſt of their fate;
From pleaſure to pleaſure they run :
Well, who cares a jot?
I envy them not
While I have my dog and my gun.

For exerciſe, air,
To the field I repair,
With ſpirits unclouded and light :
The bliſſes I find,
No ſtings leave behind,
But health and diverſion unite.

SONG XCIV.

WITH AN HONEST OLD FRIEND.

With an honeſt old friend and a merry old ſong,
And a flaſk of old port, let me ſit the night long: And 
laugh at the malice of thoſe who repine, That they 
muſt ſwig porter, While I can drink wine. 

I envy no mortal, though ever ſo great,
Nor ſcorn I a wretch for his lowly eſtate;
But what I abhor, and eſteem as a curſe,
Is poorneſs of ſpirit not poorneſs in purſe.

Then dare to be generous, dauntleſs, and gay;
Let's merrily paſs life's remainder away:
Upheld by our friends, we our foes may deſpiſe;
For the more we are envied the higher we riſe.

SONG XCV.

PLATO'S ADVICE.

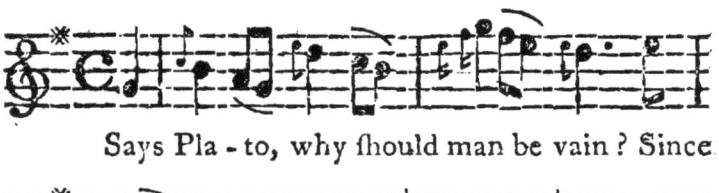

Says Pla-to, why should man be vain? Since bounteous heaven has made him great: Why looketh he with insolent disdain On those un-deck'd with wealth or state? Can splendid robes, or beds of down, Or costly gems that deck the fair; Can all the glo- - - - - - - - -

— — — — — — — — — — — — — — — ries of a crown,

Give health, or ease the brow of care?

The scepter'd king, the burthen'd slave,
    The humble, and the haughty, die;
The rich, the poor, the base, the brave,
    In dust, without distinction, lie.
Go search the tombs where monarchs rest,
    Who once the greatest titles bore:
The wealth and glory they possess'd,
    And all their honours, are no more.

So glides the meteor thro' the sky,
    And spreads along a gilded train;
But when its short-liv'd beauties die,
    Dissolves to common air again.
So 'tis with us, my jovial souls!—
    Let friendship reign while here we stay;
Let's crown our joys with flowing bowls,—
    When Jove us calls we must away.

SONG XCVI.

LOW DOWN IN THE BROOM.

My daddy is a canker'd carle, He'll nae twin wi' his gear; My minny she's a scolding wife, Hads a' the house a-steer: But let them say, or let them do, It's a' ane to me; For he's low down, he's in the broom, That's waiting on me. Waiting on me, my love, he's waiting on

me; For he's low down, he's in the broom,
That's waiting on me.

My aunty Kate fits at her wheel,
   And fair fhe lightlies me;
But weel ken I it's a' envy;
   For ne'er a jo has fhe.
      But let them fay, &c.

My coufin Kate was fair beguil'd
   Wi' Johnny i' the glen;
And ay fince-fyne fhe cries, beware
   Of falfe deluding men.
      But let her fay, &c.

Glee'd Sandy he came weft ae night,
   And fpeer'd when I faw Pate;
And ay fince-fyne the neighbours round
   They jeer me air and late.
      But let them fay, &c.

SONG XCVII.

WILLY.

When fragrant bloom of yellow broom Delights our lads and lasses, O'er yellow broom in beauty's bloom My Will all lads surpasses. Wi' Willy, then, I'll o'er the braes, I'll o'er the braes wi' Willy; Wi' Willy, then, I'll o'er the braes, I'll o'er the braes wi' Willy. From morn to eve

[Music: I'll sing the praise of buxom bonny Willy. Willy, Willy, Willy, Willy: From morn to eve I'll sing the praise of buxom bonny Willy, Willy, Willy.]

Reclin'd by Tay at noon-tide day,
  We'll pu' the daify pretty;
The live long day we'll kifs and play,
  Or fing fome loving ditty.
    Wi' Willy then, &c.

Now blithe and gay at fetting day,
  My mither dinna hinder,
I'll fing and play wi' Willy gay,
  For we twa ne'er fhall finder.
    Wi' Willy then, &c.

SONG XCVIII.

HE'S AY A KISSING ME.

I winna marry ony man but Sandy o'er the lee, I winna marry ony man but Sandy o'er the lee: I winna ha'e the dominee for guid he canna be. But I will hae my Sandy lad, my Sandy o'er the lee. For he's ay a-kissing, kissing, ay a-kissing me, He's ay a-kissing,

kiſſing, ay a-kiſſing me.

I will not have the miniſter for all his godly looks,
Nor yet will I the lawyer have, for all his wily crooks;
I will not have the plowman lad, nor yet will I the miller,
But I will have my Sandy lad without one penny filler.
        For he's aye a-kiſſing, kiſſing, &c.

I will not have the ſoldier lad for he gangs to the war,
I will not have the ſailor lad becauſe he ſmells of tar.
I will not have the lord nor laird for all their mickle gear,
But I will have my Sandy lad, my Sandy o'er the muir.
        For he's ay a-kiſſing, kiſſing, &c.

SONG XCIX.

WHEN LATE I WANDER'D.

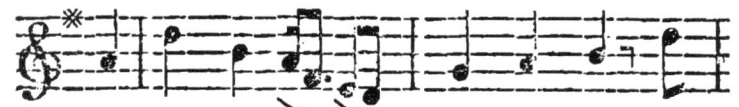

When late I wander'd o'er the plain, From nymph to nymph I strove in vain, My wild desires to rally, to rally, My wild desires to ral-ly: But now they're of themselves come home, And strange! no longer wish to roam, They centre all in Sally, in Sally, they cen-tre all in Sally.

Yet fhe, unkind one, damps my joy,
And cries, I court but to deftroy,
 Can love with ruin tally?
By thofe dear lips, thofe eyes, I fwear,
I wou'd all deaths, all torments bear,
 Rather than injure Sally.

Come then, Oh come, thou fweeter far
Than violets and rofes are,
 Or lillies of the valley;
O follow love, and quit your fear,
He'll guide you to thefe arms my dear,
 And make me bleft in Sally.

SONG C.

COME NOW ALL YE SOCIAL POW'RS.

Come now all ye focial pow'rs, Shed your influence o'er us, Crown with joy the prefent hours, En-li-ven thofe before us. Bring the flafk, the mufic bring, joy fhall quickly find us, Drink and dance, and laugh and fing, And caft dull care behind us.

Chorus.
Bring the flafk, the mufic

bring, Joy shall quickly find us, Drink and dance,

and laugh and sing, and cast dull care behind us.

  Friendship, with thy pow'r divine,
   Brighten all our features;
  What but friendship, love, and wine,
   Can make us happy creatures?
    Bring the flask, &c.

  Love, thy Godhead we adore,
   Source of generous passion;
  Nor will we ever bow before
   Those idols, wealth and fashion.
    Bring the flask, &c.

  Why should we be dull or sad,
   Since on earth we moulder?
  The grave, the gay, the good, the bad,
   They every day grow older.
    Bring the flask, &c.

  Then since time will steal away,
   'Spite of all our sorrow;
  Heighten every joy to day,
   And never mind to morrow.
    Bring the flask, &c.

SONG CI.

MY COLIN LEAVES FAIR LONDON TOWN.

My Co-lin leaves fair Lon-don town,

Its pomp, and pride, and noise ; With eager

haste he hies him down To taste of ru-

ral joys, To taste of ru - - - ral joys. Soon

as the blythsome swain's in sight, My heart

is mad with glee, I ne-ver know

fuch true delight As when he comes to me, As when he comes to me.

How fweet with him all day to rove,
    And range the meadows wide;
Nor yet lefs fweet the moon-light grove,
    All by the river's fide:
The gaudy feafons pafs away,
    How fwift when Colin's by!
How quickly glides the flow'ry May!
    How faft the Summers fly!

When Colin comes to grace the plains,
    An humble crook he bears,
He tends the flock like other fwains,
    A fhepherd quite appears.
All in the verdant month of May,
    A ruftic rake his pride,
He helps to make the new mown hay
    With Moggy by his fide.

'Gainft yellow Autumn's milder reign,
    His fickle he prepares,

He reaps the harveſt on the plain,
  All pleaſ'd with rural cares:
With jocund dance the night is crown'd,
  When all the toil is o'er,
With him I trip it on the ground,
  With bonny ſwains a ſcore.

When winter's gloomy months prevail,
  If Colin is but here,
His jovial laugh and merry tale
  For me are meikle cheer.
The folks who chooſe in towns to dwell,
  Are from my envy free,
For Moggy loves the plains too well,
  And Colin's all to me.

SONG CII.

ASK IF YON DAMASK ROSE BE SWEET.

Aſk if yon damaſk roſe be ſweet, That ſcents

the ambient air; Then aſk each ſhepherd that

you meet If dear Susanna's fair, If dear, dear Susannah's fair, If dear Susannah's fair. Ask If yon damask rose be sweet, That scents the ambient air, Then ask each shepherd that you meet, If dear Susannah's fair, If dear Susannah's fair.

Say, will the vulture leave his prey,
    And warble thro' the grove?
Bid wanton linnets quit the spray,
    Then doubt thy shepherd's love.

The spoils of war let heroes share,
Let pride in splendour shine;
Ye bards unenvy'd laurels wear,
Be fair Susannah mine.

SONG CIII.

YE MORTALS WHOM FANCIES.

Ye mortals whom fancies and troubles perplex, Whom folly misguides, and infirmities vex,  Whose lives hardly know what it is to be blest,  Who rise without joy, and lie down without rest,  Obey the glad summons, to Lethe repair, Drink deep of the stream, and forget all your care, Drink

deep of the stream, and forget all your care, Drink

deep of the stream, and forget all your care.

Old maids shall forget what they wish for in vain,
And young ones the rover they cannot regain;
The rake shall forget how last night he was cloy'd,
And Chloe again be with passion enjoy'd:
Obey then the summons, to Lethe repair,
And drink an Oblivion to trouble and care.

The wife at one draught may forget all her wants,
Or drench her fond fool, to forget her gallants;
The troubled in mind shall go chearful away,
And yesterday's wretch be quite happy to day:
Obey then the summons to Lethe repair,
Drink deep of the stream and forget all your care.

SONG CIV.

COME ROUSE FROM YOUR TRANCES.

Come rouse from your trances, the sly morn advances, To catch sluggish mortals in bed: Let the horn's jocund note In the wind sweetly float, While the fox from the brake lifts his head: Now creeping, now peeping, Now peeping, now creep-ing, The fox from the brake lifts his head. Each away to his steed, Your goddess shall lead, Come follow, my worshippers, follow, follow, follow,

follow, follow. For the chace all prepare, See

the hounds snuff the air, Hark, hark to the

huntsman's sweet hollow, hollow ; Hark to the

huntsman's sweet hollow, hollow, hollow, hol-

low, hollow.

Hark Jowler, hark Rover,
See Reynard breaks cover,
The hunters fly over the ground :

Now they fkim o'er the plain,
Now they dart down the lane,
And the hills, woods, and vallies refound.
With fplafhing and dafhing,
With fplafhing and dafhing,
The hills, woods, and vallies refound.
Then away with full fpeed,
Your goddefs fhall lead,
Come follow, my worfhippers, follow, follow, follow, follow, follow,
For the chace all prepare,
See the Hounds fnuff the air,
Hark, hark, to the huntfman's fweet hollow, hollow,
Hark to the huntfman's fweet hollow, hollow, hollow, hollow, hollow,

SONG CV.

OLD CARE BEGONE.

Old care begone, thou churlish guest, Who lov'st not flowing bowls! Thou art the miser's god a--lone; Hence, hence, we've none but souls, We've none but souls, Hence, hence, we've none but souls. Ana-cre-on bids thee quit the shrine, nor dare approach his school: For wine *inspires the soul of man, Then who would drink by ru - le. For wine inspires the soul of man, Then who would drink by rule?*

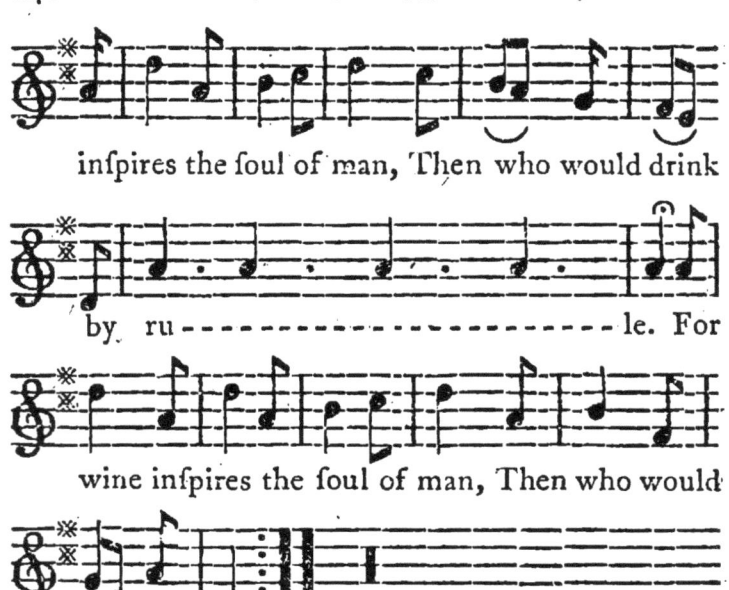

No turbid thoughts perplex the brain,
    We cynic rules decline;
Give me your joyous drinking blades,
    And cellars stor'd with wine.
With grapes my temples wreathe around,
    A hogshead striding o'er,
A rummer fill'd with generous wine,
    Ye gods, I ask no more.

In triumph then, O! how I'll quaff,
    Amidst each toping son;
I wou'd like Bacchus' self appear,
    Astride the jolly tun.

Let learned pedants rave and rail,
    Their maxims we defpife;
If fhunning wine is wifdom call'd,
    Oh! let me ne'er be wife.

The diff'rence view 'twixt fons of care,
    And lads of rofy hue,
Their fober joys are ftill the fame,
    Our drinking's ever new.
Let them go on, dream life away,
    Great Bacchus we'll adore,
And free as air we'll drink and fing,
    Till time fhall be no more.

SONG CVI.

NEVER TILL NOW I KNEW LOVE'S SMART.

Never till now I knew love's ſmart, Gueſs who it was that ſtole away my heart? 'Twas on-ly you, if you'll believe me, 'Twas only you, if you'll believe me.

Since that I've felt love's fatal pow'r,
Heavy has paſſ'd each anxious hour,
If not with you, if you'll believe me,
    If not with you, &c.
Honour and wealth no joys can bring,
Nor I be happy tho' a king,
If not with you, if you'll believe me,
    If not with you, &c.

MUSICAL MISCELLANY. 251

When from this world I'm call'd away,
For you alone I'd wiſh to ſtay,
For you alone, if you'll believe me,
   For you alone, &c.
Grave on my tomb, where'er I'm laid,
Here lies one who lov'd but one maid,
That's only you, if you'll believe me.
   That's only you, &c.

SONG CVII.

A LAUGHING SONG.

Now's the time for mirth and glee, Laugh and love and ſing with me; Cupid is my theme of ſtory, 'Tis his godſhip's fame and glory, 'Tis his godſhip's fame and glory: Ever bending to his law, Ha, ha, ha, ha, ha, ha; Ever bend-

ing to his law, ha, ha, ha, ha, ha, ha, ha, ha,

ha, ha, ha, ha, ha, ha, ha, ha, ha, ha, ha.

O'er the grave, and o'er the gay,
Cupid takes his fhare of play,
He makes heroes quite their glory,
He's the god moft fam'd in ftory,
Bending then unto his law,
Ha, ha ------------ ha

Sly the urchin deals in darts,
Without pity piercing hearts,
Cupid triumphs over paffions,
Not regarding modes nor fafhions,
Firmly fix'd is Cupids law.
Ha, ha----------- ha

You may doubt thefe things are true;
But they're facts 'twixt me and you,

MUSICAL MISCELLANY. 253

Then young men and maids be wary,
How ye meet before ye marry,
Cupid's will is folely law.
Ha ha- - - - - - - - - - - ha.

SONG CVIII.

COME ROUSE BROTHER SPORTSMAN.

Come rouse, brother sportsman, The hunters  all cry, We've got a strong scent, and a favoring sky, We've got a strong scent, we've got  a strong scent, we've got a strong scent and  a favouring sky. The horns sprightly notes,

Vol. II.   X

And the lark's early song, Will chide the dull sportsman for sleeping so long, Will chi — — — — — — — — — — — — — — de, Will chide the dull sportsman for sleeping so long, Will chide the dull sportsman for sleeping so long.

Bright Phœbus has shewn us the glimpse of his face.
Peep'd in at our windows and call'd to the chace,

He foon will be up, for his dawn wears away,
And makes the fields blufh with the beams of his ray,
Sweet Molly may teize you perhaps to lie down,
And if you refufe her, perhaps fhe may frown;
But tell her fweet love muft to hunting give place,
For as well as her charms, there are charms in the chace.

Look yonder, look yonder, old Reynard I fpy,
At his brufh nimbly follows brifk Chanter and Fly:
They feize on their prey, fee his eye balls they roll,
We're in at the death, now go home to the bowl.
There we'll fill up our glaffes and toaft to the king,
From a bumper frefh loyalty ever will fpring,
To George, peace and glory may heavens difpenfe,
And fox-hunters flourifh a thoufand years hence.

SONG CIX.

THE FRIENDS.

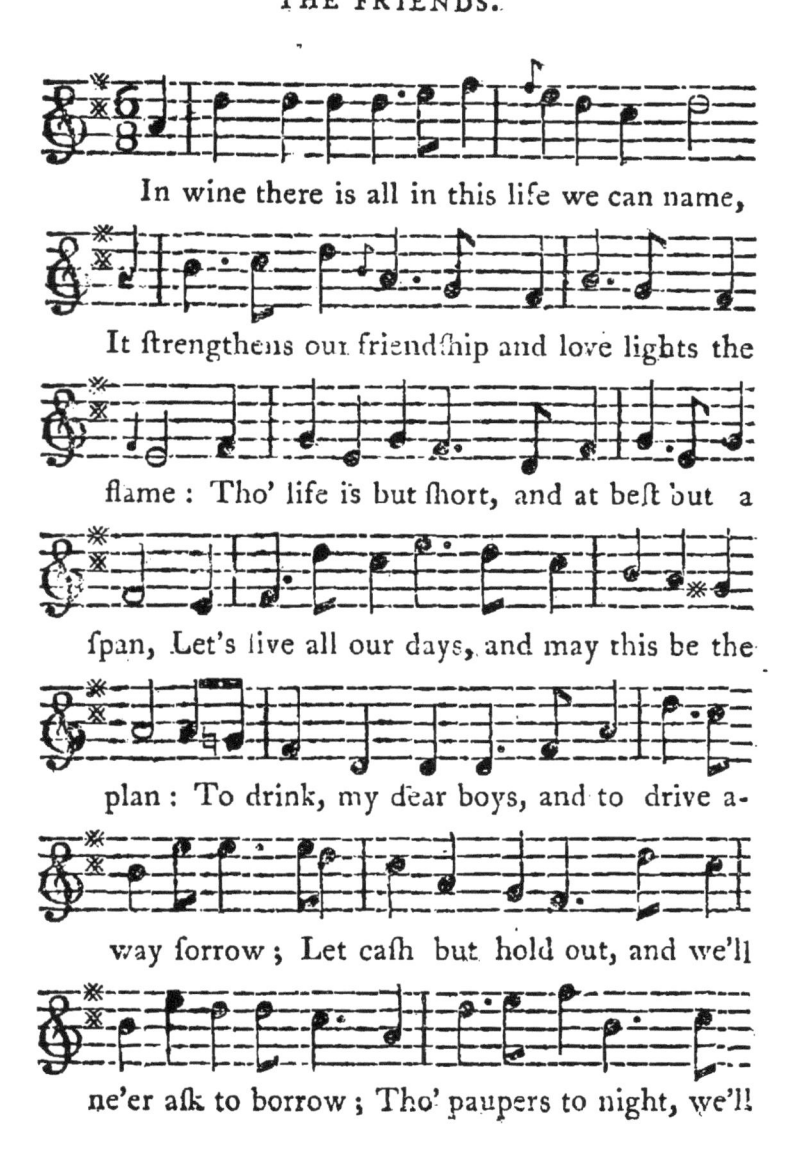

In wine there is all in this life we can name,

It strengthens our friendship and love lights the

flame: Tho' life is but short, and at best but a

span, Let's live all our days, and may this be the

plan: To drink, my dear boys, and to drive a-

way sorrow; Let cash but hold out, and we'll

ne'er ask to borrow; Tho' paupers to night, we'll

be rich rogues to-morrow, be rich rogues to-morrow, be rich rogues to morrow; Tho' paupers to-night, we'll be rich rogues to-morrow.

In a neat country village; yet not far from town,
A clean bed for a friend whene'er he comes down,
With a choice pack of hounds us to wake in the morn,
A hunter for each to fet off with the horn.
  Then drink, &c.

Our difhes well chofen, and nice in their fort,
Our cellars well ftor'd with good claret and port,
A bumper to hail, to hail the all glorious,
Our grandfires did fo, and our fathers before us.
  Then drink, &c.

A jolly brifk chaplain that can well grace the table,
Who will drink like a man as long as he's able,

Who'll drink till his face port and claret makes red,
Then ſtagger enlighten'd quite happy to bed.
  Then drink, &c.

May each man have a laſs, that he wiſhes would prove
To his honour moſt true, and ſincere to his love,
With beauty, with wit, to change never prone,
And the bandage good-nature to bind us their own.
  Then drink, &c.

And juſt as we've liv'd may we cloſe the laſt ſcene,
Quite free from all trouble, quite free from all pain,
The young they may wonder, the old they may ſtare,
And lift up their hands, ſay what friendſhip was there?
  Then drink, &c.

SONG CX.

I MADE LOVE TO KATE.

I made love to Kate, long I ſigh'd for ſhe,
Till I heard of late, ſhe'd a mind to me. me.

I met her on the green, in her best array, So pretty she did seem, she stole my heart away: Oh then we kiss'd and prest, were we much to blame? Had you been in my place, why you had done the same. Oh! same.

As I fonder grew, she began to prate,
Quoth she, I'll marry you, and you will marry Kate.
    But then I laugh'd and swore,
        I lov'd her more than so,
    Ty'd each to a rope's end,
        Is tugging to and fro.

Again we kifs'd and preft, were we much to blame?
Had you been in my place, why you had done the fame.

Then fhe figh'd, and faid, fhe was won'l'rous fick;
Dicky Katy led, Katy fhe led Dick;
    Long we toy'd and play'd
       Under yonder oak,
    Katy loft the game,
       Tho' fhe play'd in Joke,
For there we did, alas! what I dare not name,
Had you been in my place, why you had done the fame.

SONG CXI.

AS SURE AS A GUN.

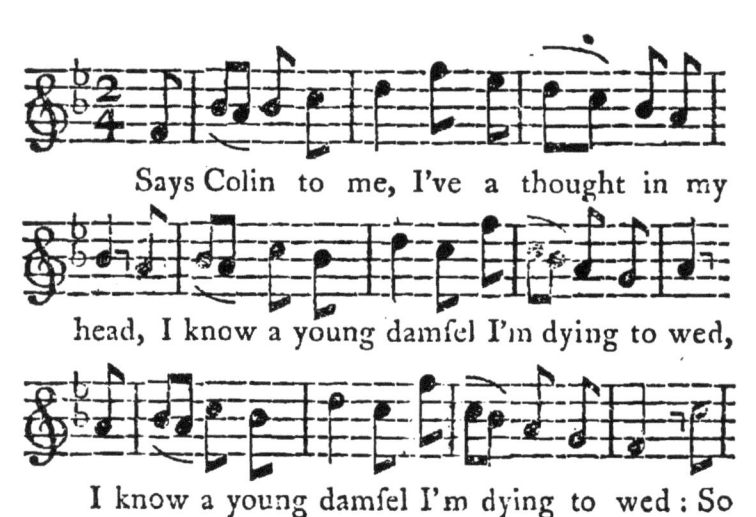

Says Colin to me, I've a thought in my head, I know a young damfel I'm dying to wed, I know a young damfel I'm dying to wed: So please you, quoth I, and whene'er it is done,

You'll quarrel and you'll part again, as sure as

a gun, As sure as a gun, As sure as a gun,

You'll quarrel and you'll part again, as sure as

a gun.

And so when you're married (poor amorous wight!)
You'll bill it and coo it from morning till night;
But trust me, good Colin, you'll find it bad fun—
Instead of which you'll fight and scratch—as sure as
    a gun!
But shou'd she prove fond of her nown dearest love,
And you be as souple, and soft as her glove;

262   THE EDINBURGH

Yet be fhe a faint, and as chafte as a nun—
You're faften'd to her apron-ftrings—as fure as a
    gun!
Suppofe it was you, then, faid he with a leer;
You wou'd not ferve me fo, I'm certain, my dear:
In troth I replied, I will anfwer for none—
But do as other women do—as fure as a gun!

SONG CXII.
THE BIRD'S NEST.

I've found out a gift for my fair, I've found where the wood-pigeons breed, But let me that plunder forbear, She'll fay it's a bar-ba-rous deed; But let me that plunder forbear, She'll say its a bar - - - barous deed.

For he ne'er can be true, she averr'd,
Who can rob a poor bird of its young;
And I lov'd her the more, when I heard
Such tenderness fall from her tongue.

I've heard her with sweetness unfold,
How that pity was due to a Dove:
That it ever attended the bold,
And she call'd it the sister of Love.

SONG CXIII.

NOW PHOEBUS SINKETH IN THE WEST.

Now Phoebus finketh in the weft, Welcome fong and welcome jeft, Midnight fhout and revelry, Tipfy dance and jollity, Midnight fhout and revelry, Tipfy dance and jollity. Now Phœbus finketh in the weft, Welcome fong and welcome jeft, Midnight fhout and revelry,

Tipsy dance and jollity. Braid your locks, with rosy twine, dropping odours, dropping wine, Braid your lo----------cks with rosy twine, dropping odours, dropping wine, dropping odours, dropping wine, dropping odours, dropping wine. Rigour now is gone to bed, And advice with scrup'lous head, Strict age and sour severi-ty, With their grave faws in flumber ly,

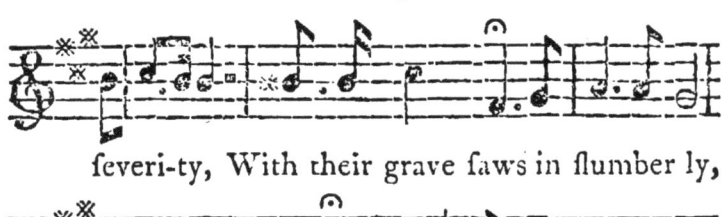

With their grave faws in flumber ly. *Da Capo.*

SONG CXIV.

THE LITTLE MAN AND LITTLE MAID.

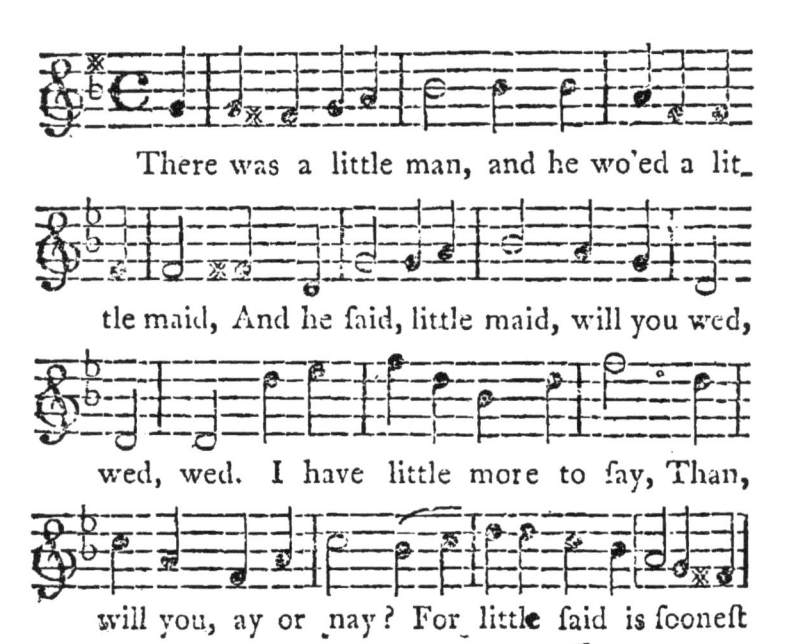

There was a little man, and he wo'ed a lit_

tle maid, And he faid, little maid, will you wed,

wed, wed. I have little more to fay, Than,

will you, ay or nay? For little faid is fooneft

mend - ed - ed.

Then reply'd the little maid, little fir, you've little faid
   To induce a little maid, to wed, wed, wed,
You muft fay a little more, and produce a little dow'r,
   Ere I make a little print in your bed, bed, bed,

Then the little man replied, if you'll be my little bride
   I'll raife my love a little higher;
Tho' I little love to prate, my little heart is great,
   With the little god of love all on fire.

Then the little maid replied, fhould I be your little bride,
   Pray what fhall we do for to eat, eat, eat?
Will the flame that you're fo rich in ferve for fire in the kitchen?
   Or the little god of love turn the fpit, fpit, fpit?

Then the little man he figh'd, fome fay a little cried,
   For his little breaft was big with forrow;
I am your little flave, if the little that I have
   Is too little, little dear, I will borrow.

So the little man fo gent, made the little maid relent,
   And fet her little heart a thinking,
Tho' his offers were but fmall, fhe took his little all,
   And could have of a cat but her fkin.

SONG CXV.

NOBODY.

If to force me to sing it be your intention,

Some one I will hint at, yet nobody mention,

Nobody you'll cry, pshaw, that must be stuff,

At singing I'm no-bo-dy, that's the first proof,

No, no-bo-dy, no, no-bo-dy, no-bo-dy,

nobody, no-bo-dy, no.

Nobody's a name every body will own,
When something they ought to be asham'd of have
   done;
'Tis a name well applied to old maids and young
   beaus,
What they were intended for nobody knows.
           No, nobody, &c.

If negligent servants should china-plate crack,
The fault is still laid on poor nobody's back;
If accidents happen at home or abroad,
When nobody's blam'd for it, is not that odd?
           No, nobody, &c.

Nobody can tell you the tricks that are play'd,
When nobody's by, betwixt master and maid:
She gently crys out, sir, there'll some body hear us,
He softly replies, my dear, nobody's near us.
           No, nobody, &c.

But big with child proving, she's quickly discarded,
When favours are granted, nobody's rewarded;
And when she's examined, crys, mortals, forbid it,
If I'm got with child, it was nobody did it.
           No, nobody, &c.

When by stealth, the gallant, the wanton wife leaves,
The husband's affrighten'd, and thinks it is thieves;

He rouses himself, and crys loudly who's there?
The wife pats his cheek, and says, nobody, dear.
   No, nobody, &c.

Enough now of nobody sure has been sung,
Since nobody's mention'd, nor nobody's wrong'd;
I hope for free speaking I may not be blam'd,
Since nobody's injur'd, nor nobody's nam'd,
   No, nobody, &c.

SONG CXVI.

FY GAR RUB HER OE'R WI' STRAE.

And gin ye meet a bonny laffie, Gie'er a kifs, and let her gae; But if ye meet a dir-ty huffy, Fy gar rub her o'er wi' ftrae. Be fure ye dinna quit the grip Of ilka joy when ye are young, Before auld age your vi-tals nip, And lay you twafauld o'er a rung.

Sweet youth's a blithe and heartſome time ;
    Then lads and laſſes, while 'tis May,
Gae pu' the gowan in it's prime
    Before it wither and decay.
Watch the faft minutes of delyte,
    When Jenny ſpeaks beneath her breath,
And kiſſes, laying a' the wyte
    On you if ſhe kepp ony ſkaith.

Haith ye're ill-bred, ſhe'll ſmiling ſay,
    Ye'll worry me, ye greedy rook :
Syne frae your arms ſhe'll rin away,
    And hide herſelf in ſome dark nook.
Her laugh will lead you to the place
    Where lies the happineſs ye want,
And plainly tell you to your face
    Nineteen na-ſays are ha'f a grant.

Now to her heaving boſom cling
    And ſweetly toolie for a kiſs :
Upon her finger whoop a ring,
    As taiken of a future bliſs.
Theſe benniſons, I'm very ſure,
    Are of the gods indulgent grant :
Then, ſurly carls, whiſht, forbear
    To plague us with your whining cant.

SONG CXVII.
To the foregoing Tune.

Dear Roger, if your Jenny geck
   And anfwer kindnefs wi' a flight,
Seem unconcern'd at her neglect;
   For women in a man delight;
But them defpife who're foon defeat,
   And wi' a fimple face give way:
To a repulfe then be not blate;
   Pufh bauldly on and win the day.

When maidens, innocently young,
   Say aften what they never mean,
Ne'er mind their pretty lying tongue,
   But tent the language of their een:
If thefe agree, and fhe perfift
   To anfwer a' your love with hate,
Seek elfewhere to be better bleft,
   And let her figh when its too late.

SONG CXVIII.

AH WHY MUST WORDS.

Ah why muft words my flame reveal? What needs my Damon bid my tell What all my actions prove? What all my actions prove.

A blufh whene'er I meet his eye, When e'er I hear his name A figh betrays my fecret love, - - - - - betrays my fecret love.

In all their sports upon the plain
My eyes still fix'd on him remain,
 And him alone approve;
The rest unheeded, dance or play,
He steals from all my praise away,
 And can he doubt my love?

Whene'er we meet, my looks confess
The pleasures which my soul possess,
 And all it's cares remove.
Still, still too short appears his stay,
I frame excuses for delay,
 Can this be ought but love?

Does any speak in Damon's praise,
How pleas'd am I with all he says,
 And every word approve;
Is he defam'd, tho' but in jest,
I feel resentment fire my breast,
 Alas! because I love.

But O! what tortures tear my heart,
When I suspect his looks impart
 The least desire to rove.
I hate the maid who gives me pain,
Yet him I strive to hate in vain,
 For ah! that hate is love.

Then ask not words, but read my eyes,
Believe my blushes, trust my sighs,

All thefe my paffion prove:
Words may deceive, may fpring from art,
But the true language of my heart
To Damon muft be love.

SONG CXIX.

WINTER.

A-dieu, ye groves, adieu ye plains, All na-
ture mourning lies. See gloomy clouds, and 
thick'ning rains Obfcure the lab'ring fkies. 
See, fee, from a-far, th'im-pend-ing ftorm With

fullen hafte ap - - pear, See win-ter comes, A
drea - ry form, to rule - - - the falling year.

No more the lambs with gamefome bound,
    Rejoice the gladden'd fight :
No more the gay enamell'd ground,
    Or fylvan fcenes delight.
Thus, lovely Nancy, much lov'd maid,
    Thy early charms muft fail ;
Thy rofe muft droop, the lilly fade,
    And winter foon prevail.

Again the lark, fweet bird of day,
    May rife on active wings,
Again the fportive herds may play,
    And hail reviving fpring.
But youth, my fair, fees no return,
    The pleafing bubble's o'er,
In vain it's fleeting joys you mourn,
    They fall to bloom no more.

Hafte, then, dear girl, the time improve,
    Which art can ne'er regain,
In blifsfull fcenes of mutual love,
    With fome diftinguifh'd fwain ;

So shall life's spring, like jocund May,
  Pass smiling and serene;
Thus summer, autumn, glide away,
  And winter soon prevail.

SONG CXX.

BONNY JEAN.

Love's goddess in a myr-tle grove, Said, Cupid, bend thy bow with speed, Nor let thy shaft at random rove, For Jen--ny's haughty heart must bled. The smiling boy with di--

vine art, From Paphos ſhot an ar-row keen,

Which flew un-erring to the heart, And kill'd

the pride of bon-ny Jean.

No more the nymph, with haughty air,
Refuſes Willy's kind addreſs;
Her yielding bluſhes ſhow no care,
But too much fondneſs to ſuppreſs.
No more the youth is ſullen now,
But looks the gayeſt on the green,
Whilſt every day he ſpies ſome new
Surprizing charms in bonny Jean.

A thouſand tranſports crowd his breaſt,
He moves as light as fleeting wind;
His former ſorrows ſeem a jeſt,
Now when his Jenny is turn'd kind.
Riches he looks on with diſdain,
The glorious fields of war look mean;

The chearful hound and horn gives pain;
If abfent from his bonny Jean.

The day he fpends in am'rous gaze,
Which ev'n in fummer fhort'ned feems;
When funk in downs, with glad amaze,
He wonders at her in his dreams.
All charms difclos'd, fhe looks more bright
Than Troy's prize, the Spartan Queen.
With breaking day, he lifts his fight,
And pants to be with bonny Jean.

SONG CXXI.
WHY HANGS THAT CLOUD.

Why hangs that cloud u - pon thy brow?

That beauteous heaven erewhile ferene: Whence

do thefe ftorms and tempefts flow? Or wha

MUSICAL MISCELLANY. 281

this guft of paffion mean? And muft then
mankind lofe that light, Which in thine eyes
was wont to fhine? And ly obfcur'd in
end-lefs night, For each poor fil-ly speech
of mine?

Dear child, how can I wrong thy name,
 Since 'tis acknowledged at all hands,
That could ill tongues abufe thy fame,
 Thy beauty can make large amends;
Or if I durft profanely try
 Thy beauty's pow'rful charms t' upbraid,
Thy virtue well might give the lie,
 Nor call thy beauty to it's aid.

For Venus every heart t' enfnare,
  With all her charms has deck'd thy face,
And Pallas with unufual care,
  Bids wifdom heighten every grace.
Who can the double pain endure!
  Or who muft not refign the field
To thee, celeftial maid, fecure
  With Cupid's bow, and Pallas fhield?

If then to thee fuch pow'r is given,
  Let not a wretch in torment live,
But fmile, and learn to copy heaven,
  Since we muft fin ere it forgive.
Yet pitying heaven not only does
  Forgive th' offender and th' offence,
But even itfelf appeas'd beftows,
  As the reward of penitence.

SONG CXXII.

THE DUSKY NIGHT,

The dusky night rides down the sky, And ushers in the morn; The hounds all join in jovial cry, The hounds all join in jovial cry, The huntsman winds his horn, The huntsman winds his horn. And a hunting we will go, A hunting we will go, A hunting we will go ---- A hunting we will go. And a hunting we will

go, A hunting we will go, And hunting we
will go --- A hunting we will go.

The wife around her husband throws
    Her arms to make him stay :
My dear, it rains, it hails, it blows,
    You cannot hunt to-day.
        Yet a hunting, &c.

Sly Reynard now like light'ning flies,
    And sweeps across the vale ;
But when the hounds too near he spies,
    He drops his bushy tail.
        Then a hunting, &s.

Fond echo seems to like the sport,
    And join the jovial cry ;
The woods and hills the sound retort,
    And music fills the sky,
        When a hunting, &c.

At last his strength to faintness worn,
    Poor Reynard ceases flight ;

Then hungry homeward we return
   To feaſt away the night.
     And a drinking, &c.

Ye jovial hunters in the morn
   Prepare then for the chace;
Riſe at the ſounding of the horn,
   And health with ſport embrace,
     When a hunting, &c.

SONG CXXIII.

THE BONNY SCOTMAN.

Ye gales that gently wave the sea, And please the canny boatman, Bear me frae hence, or bring to me, My blyth, my bonny Scotman, Bear me frae hence, or bring to me, My blyth my bonny Scotman, my blyth my bonny Scotman. In holy bands we join'd our hands, Yet may not that difcover, While parents rate a large eftate before a faith-ful lo-ver. In holy bands we join'd our hands, Yet may not that difcover, While parents rate a large eftate be-fore a faithful lo-ver, before a faithful lo-ver, before a faith-ful lo-ver; While parents rate a large eftate be-fore a faithful lover.

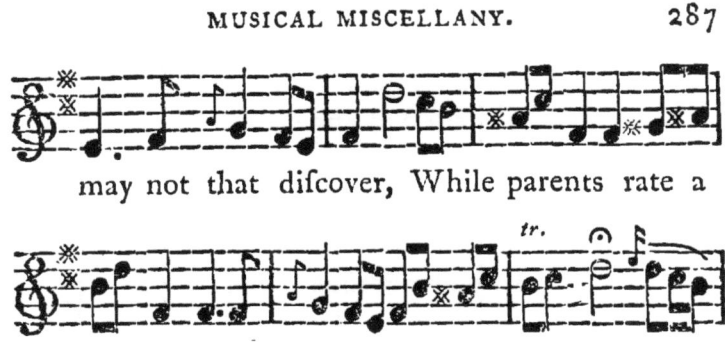

But I wou'd chuse in Highland glens,
   To herd the kid and goat man ;
E'er I cou'd for such little ends,
   Refuse my bonny Scotman.
Wae worth the man who first began,
   The base ungen'rous fashion ;
From greedy views, love's art to use,
   Whilst stranger to it's passion.

Frae foreign fields my lovely youth,
   Haste to thy longing lassie ;
Who pants to kiss thy balmy mouth,
   And in her bosom press thee :
Love gives the word, then haste on board,
   Fair wind and gentle boatman,
Waft o'er, waft o'er, from yonder shore.
   My blyth my bonny Scotman.

SONG CXXIV.

THE SPINNING WHEEL.

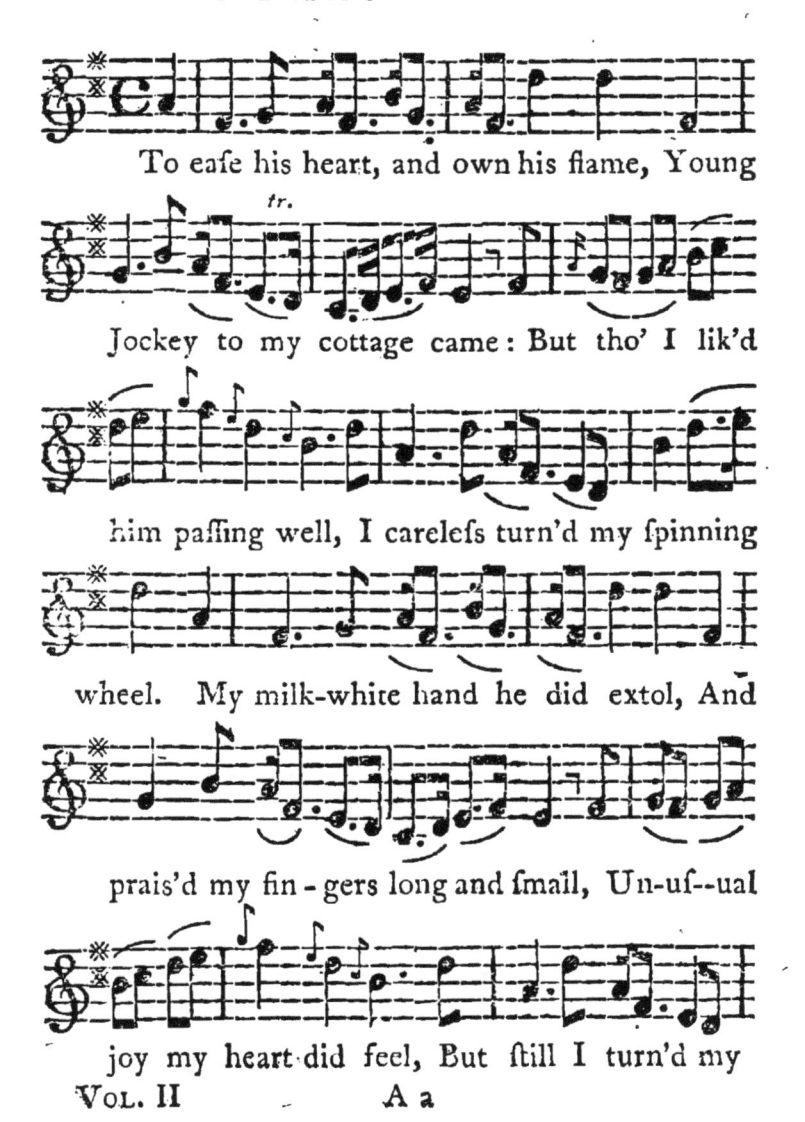

To eafe his heart, and own his flame, Young Jockey to my cottage came: But tho' I lik'd him paffing well, I carelefs turn'd my fpinning wheel. My milk-white hand he did extol, And prais'd my fin-gers long and fmall, Un-uf-ual joy my heart did feel, But ftill I turn'd my spinning wheel. Then round about my slender

waist He clasp'd his arms, and me embrac'd,

To kiss my hand he down did kneel, But yet

I turn'd my spin-ning wheel. With gentle voice

I bid him rise; He bless'd my neck, my lips

and eyes; My fondness I could scarce conceal,

Yet still I turn'd my spinning wheel. Till

bolder grown, so close he prest, His wanton thoughts I quickly guess'd, Then push'd him from my rock and reel, And angry turn'd my spin--ning wheel. At last, when I be-gan to chide, He swore he meant me for his bride: 'Twas then my love I did re---veal, And flung a-way my spinning wheel.

SONG CXXV.

THE POWER OF MUSIC.

When Orpheus went down to the regions be-

low, Which men are forbidden to fee; He tun'd

up his lyre, as old hifto-ries fhew, To fet his

Eurydice free, To fet his Eury-dice free. All

hell was aftonifh'd a perfon fo wife Should rafh-

ly endanger his life, And venture fo far; But

how vaft their furprife! When they heard that he came for his wife! How vaft their furprife! When they heard that he came for his wife!

To find out a punifhment due to his fault,
  Old Pluto long puzzled his brain;
But hell had not torments fufficient, he thought;
  So he gave him his wife back again.
But pity fucceeding found place in his heart;
  And, pleas'd with his playing fo well,
He took her again in reward of his art;
  Such merit had mufic in hell!

SONG CXXVI.

DIOGENES SURLY AND PROUD.

Di-o-ge-nes furly and proud, Who fnarl'd at the Macedon youth, Delighted in wine that was good, Becaufe in good wine there is truth; But growing as poor as a Job, And un-a-ble to pur-chafe a flafk, He chofe for his manfion a tub, And liv'd by the fcent of his ca- - - - - - - -

— — — — — — — — — fk, And liv'd by the fcent

of his cafk.

Heraclitus would never deny
    A bumper to cherifh his heart;
And, when he was maudlin, would cry;
    Becaufe he had empty'd his quart:
Though fome were fo foolifh to think
    He wept at men's folly and vice,
When 'twas only his cuftom to drink
    'Till the liquor ran out at his eyes.

Democritus always was glad
    To tipple and cherifh his foul;
Would laugh like a man that was mad,
    When over a jolly full bowl:
While his cellar with wine was well ftor'd,
    His liquor he'd merrily quaff;
And, when he was drunk as a lord,
    At thofe that were fober he'd laugh,

Copernicus, too, like the reft,
    Believ'd there was wifdom in wine:
And knew that a cup of the beft
    Made reafon the brighter to fhine:

With wine he replenifh'd his veins,
  And made his philofophy reel:
Then fancy'd the world, as his brains,
  Turn'd round like a chariot wheel.

Ariftotle, that mafter of arts,
  Had been but a dunce without wine;
For what we afcribe to his parts,
  Is due to the juice of the vine;
His belly, fome authors agree,
  Was as big as a watering-trough:
He therefore leap'd into the fea,
  Becaufe he'd have liquor enough.

When Pyrrho had taken a glafs,
  He faw that no object appear'd
Exactly the fame as it was
  Before he had liquor'd his beard;
For things running round in his drink,
  Which fober he motionlefs found,
Occafion'd the fceptic to think
  There was nothing of truth to be found.

Old Plato was reckon'd divine,
  Who wifely to virtue was prone;
But, had it not been for good wine,
  His merit had never been known:
By wine we are generous made;
  It furnifhes fancy with wings;
Without it we ne'er fhould have had
  Philofophers, poets, or kings.

SONG CXXVII.

M'GREGOR ARUARO.

From the chace in the mountain as I was returning, By the side of a fountain Malrina sat mourning; To the winds that loud whistl'd she told her sad story; And the vallies re-echoed MacGregor A-ruaro.

Like a flash of red lightning o'er the heath came Macara.
More fleet than the roe-buck on the lofty Beinn-lara.

Oh where is M'Gregor? say, where does he hover?
You son of bold Calmar, why tarries my lover?

Then the voice of soft sorrow, from his bosom thus
    sounded,
Low lies your M'Gregor, pale, mangl'd and wounded,
Overcome with deep slumber, to the rock I convey'd
    him,   (tray'd him.
Where the sons of black malice to his foes have be-

As the blast from the mountain soon nips the fresh
    blossom,
So died the fair bud of fond hope in her bosom;
M'Gregor! M'Gregor! loud echoes resounded;
And the hills rung in pity, M'Gregor is wounded!

Near the brook in the valley the green turf did hide
    her;   (her;
And they laid down M'Gregor sound sleeping beside
Secure is their dwelling from foes and black slander;
Near the loud roaring waters their spirits oft wander.

SONG CXXVIII.

THE SAILOR'S ALLEGORY.

Life's like a ship, in conftant motion, fometimes high and fometimes low; where ev'ry one muft brave the ocean, What-fo-e-ver wind may blow: If, unaffail'd by fquall or fhow-er. Wafted by the gentle gales; Let's not lofe the fav'ring hour, While fuccefs attends our fails.

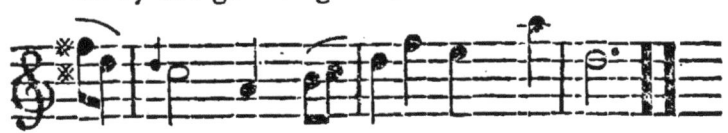

Or, if the wayward winds should bluster,
    Let us not give way to fear;
But let us all our Patience muster,
    And learn, by Reason, how to steer:
Let Judgment keep you ever steady,
    'Tis a ballast never fails;
Should dangers rise, be ever ready,
    To manage well the swelling sails.

Trust not too much your own opinion,
    While your vessel's under way;
Let good example bear dominion,
    That's a compass will not stray:
When thund'ring tempests make you shudder,
    Or Boreas on the surface rails;
Let good Discretion guide the rudder,
    And Providence attend the sails.

Then, when you're safe from danger, riding
    In some welcome port or bay;
Hope be the anchor you confide in,
    And Care, awhile, enslumber'd lay:
Or, when each cann, with liquor flowing,
    And good fellowship prevails;
Let each true heart, with rapture glowing,
    Drink " success unto our sails."

SONG CXXIX.
THE LIQUOR OF LIFE.

Recit.

While here Anacreon's chosen sons combine,

Like him to taste the joys of mirth and wine;

While the full bowl is with the goblet crown'd,

Harmonic let the joyful song resound: To

banish life's troubles the Grecian old sage Press'd

the juice of the vintage oft into the bowl, Press'd

the juice of the vintage oft into the bowl: It

made him forget all the cares of old age, It

bloom'd in his face, and made happy his soul,

It bloom'd in his face and made happy his soul,

It bloom'd in his face and made hap-py his soul·

Quick.

While here, then, we're found, push the bottle

around, While here, then, we're found, push the

bottle around, 'Tis the liquor of life, 'Tis the liquor of life, 'tis the liquor of life, No care can

controul.

This jovial philofopher taught that the fun
Was thirſty, and oft took a ſwig from the main;
The planets would tipple as faſt as they run;
The earth, too, was dry, and would ſuck up the rain,
    While here then we're found,
    Puſh the bottle around,—
'Tis the liquor of life, pray who can refrain?

SONG CXXX.

ROBIN ADAIR.

You're welcome to Pax-ton, Robin Adair:

How does Johnny Mackrill do? Aye, and Luke

Gard'ner too? Why did they no come with you'

Robin Adair? Come, and fit down by me,

Robin Adair; And welcome you shall be To

every thing that you see: Why did they not

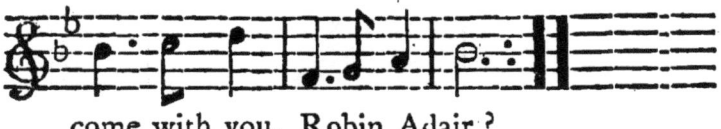

come with you, Robin Adair?

I will drink wine with you, Robin Adair,
I will drink wine with you, Robin Adair;
   Rum-punch, aye, or brandy to,
   By my foul I'll get drunk with you;
Why did they not come with you, Robin Adair?

Then let us drink about, Robin Adair,
Then let us drink about, Robin Adair,
   Till we've drank a Hogfhead out,
   Then we'll be fow nae doubt;
Why did they not come with you, Robin Adair?

SONG CXXXI.

WITHIN A MILE OF EDINBURGH.

'Twas with-in a mile of Edinburgh town,

In the ro-fy time of the year, fweet

flow-ers bloom'd, and the grafs was down,

And each fhepherd woed his dear: Bonny Jock-

ey, blyth and gay, Kifs'd fweet Jenny making

hay: The laffie blufh'd, and frowning cry'd, No,

no, it will not do; I cannot, cannot, won-

not, wonnot, mannot buckle too.

Jockey was a wag that never would wed,
   Tho' long he had follow'd the lafs,
Contented fhe earn'd and eat her brown bread,
   And merrily turn'd up the grafs:
     Bonny Jockey, blyth and free,
     Won her heart right merily,
Yet ftill fhe blufh'd, and frowning cry'd, no, no, it
   will not do,
I cannot cannot, wonnot wonnot, mannot buckle too.

But when he vow'd he wou'd make her his bride,
   Tho' his flocks and herds were not few,
She gave him her hand, and a kifs befide,
   And vow'd fhe'd for ever be true;
     Bonny Jockey, blyth and free,
     Won her heart right merrily,
At church fhe no more frowning cry'd, no, no, it
   will not do,
I cannot cannot, wonnot wonnot, mannot buckle too.

SONG XXXII.

IN FORMER TIMES WE FRANCE DID ROUT,

In former times we France did rout, 'Cauſe

then our princes drank old ſtout; But now, even

men of low degree, Drink what thoſe drank whom

we made flee. I'll bet my beſt mi-li-tia gun, Who

drinks like them, like them will run: For ſure no

knight was ever born Compar'd to Sir John Barley-corn. With a hey gee, wo gee, up gee wo,

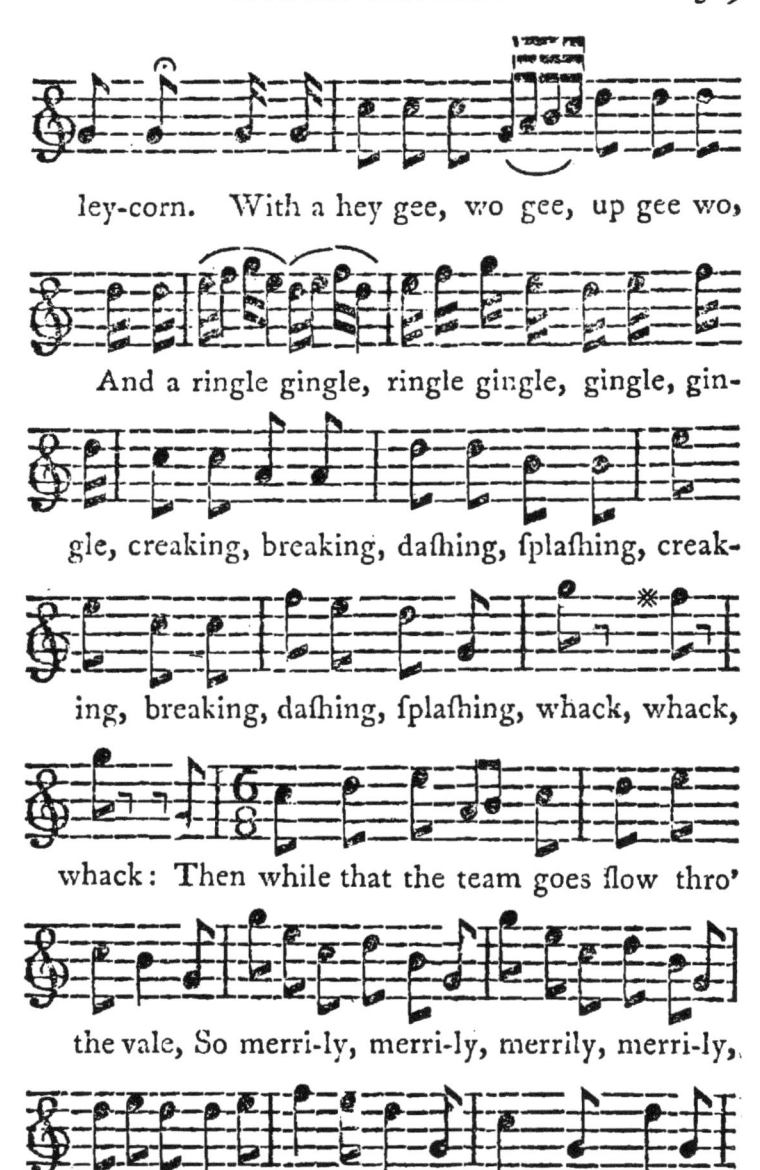

And a ringle gingle, ringle gingle, gingle, gin-

gle, creaking, breaking, dafhing, fplafhing, creak-

ing, breaking, dafhing, fplafhing, whack, whack,

whack: Then while that the team goes flow thro'

the vale, So merri-ly, merri-ly, merrily, merri-ly,

merri-ly let us wet a lip, For Joan fhe loves a

smack of the whip, and the smack of nut-brown

ale.

I ne'er want bolus, draught, or pill,
For 'tis outlandish liquors kill;
I keep to ale, and ale keeps me
From ev'ry ail, but hiccups, free;
Nay, on my beast, the same I try,
So Dobbin is as stout as I,
For sure no Doctor e'er was born,
Compar'd to Sir John Barley-corn.
    With a hey gee wo, &c.

SONG XXXIII.

DEAR IMAGE OF THE MAID I LOVE.

Dear i-mage of the maid I love, Whoſe

charms you bring to view; In ab-ſence ſome de-

light I feel, By gazing ſtill on you; De-

barr'd her ſight, by tyrant power, How wretched

wretched ſhould I be, But that I chear each

lonely hour, by gazing ſtill on thee, by gazing

ſtill on thee, by gaz-ing ſtill on thee.

Oh! cou'd I call this fair one mine,
   What rapture ſhou'd I feel;
Oh! cou'd I preſs that form divine,
   Each hour my bleſs wou'd feal:

But ah! deprived of all her charms,
   My foul can find no reſt:
And ſhou'd ſhe bleſs another's arms,
   Deſpair wou'd fill my breaſt.

SONG CXXXIV.

POOR SILLY FAN.

The fields were gay, and sweet the hay, Our gypsies sat upon the grass; Both lad and lass by you were fed, 'Twas all to cheat poor silly Fan. The fields were gay, and sweet the hay, Our gypsies sat upon the grass, upon the grass: Both lad and lass by you were fed, by you were fed, 'Twas all to cheat poor fil - - ly Fan.

Whene'er we meet, with kiffes fweet;
With fpeeches foft you won my heart;
The hawthorn bufh fhou'd make you blufh,
'Twas there you did betray my heart.

SONG CXXXV.

BATCHELORS HALL.

To Batchelors hall we good fellows invite,
To partake of the chace, that makes up our delight: We have spirits like fire, and of health such a stock, That our pulse strikes the seconds as true as a clock: Did you see us you'd swear, as we mount with a grace; Did you see us you'd

swear, As we mount with a grace, That Di-a-na

had dubb'd some new gods of the chace, That

Di-a-na had dubb'd some new gods of the chace.

Hark a-way, hark away, All nature looks gay,

And Aurora with smiles ush-ers in the bright day.

Dick Thickset came mounted upon a fine black,
A better fleet gelding ne'er hunter did back:
Tom Trig rode a bay, full of mettle and bone,
And gayly Bob Buxon rode proud on a roan;
But the horse of all horses that rivall'd the day,
Was the Squire's Neck-or-nothing, and that was a
    grey.

Hark away, hark away,
While our spirits are gay,
Let us drink to the joys of the next coming day.

Then for hounds there was Nimble, so well that climbs rocks,
And Cocknose, a good one at scenting a Fox,
Little Plunge, like a mole, who with ferret and search,
And beetle-browed Hawks-eye, so dead at a lurch:
Young Sly-looks, that scents the strong breeze from the South,
And musical Echo-well, with his deep mouth.
 Hark away, &c.

Our horses, thus all of the very best blood,
'Tis not likely you'll easily find such a stud;
And for hounds our opinions with thousands we'll back, (pack:
That all England throughout can't produce such a
Thus having described you dogs, horses, and crew,
Away we set off, for the Fox is in view.
 Hark away, &c.

Sly Reynard's brought home, while the horns sound a call,
And now you're all welcome to Bachelor's hall
The savory Sir-loin grateful smoaks on the board,
And Bacchus pours wine from his favourite hoard;
Come on then, do honour to this jovial place. (chace.
And enjoy the sweet pleasures that spring from the
 Hark away, &c.

SONG CXXXVI.

COTCHELIN SAT ALL ALONE.

Cotchelin sat all alone, Not a soul beside her, While from Teddy, who was gone, Oceans did divide her. His pipes which she'd been us'd to hear, Careless left behind him: She thought she'd try her woes to chear, Till once again she'd find him. 'Twill not do, you loodle loo, Arrah, now be easy! Ted was born with grief to make Cotchelin run cra-zy.

> She takes them up and lays them down,
> And now her bosom's panting;
> And now she'd sigh, and now she'd frown,
> For Teddy still was wanting;
> And now she plays her pipes again,
> The pipes of her dear Teddy,
> And makes them tune his fav'rite strain,
> Arrah, be easy Paddy!
> Ah! 'twill not do you loodle loo,
> Arrah! now be easy,
> Ted was born with grief to make,
> Cotchelin run crazy.

> Teddy from behind a bush,
> Where he'd long been list'ning;
> Now like light'ning forth did rush,
> His eyes with pleasure glist'ning,
> Snatching up the pipes he play'd,
> Pouring out his pleasure,
> Whilst half delighted, half afraid,
> Kate the time did measure,
> Ah that will do, my loodle loo,
> Arrah! now I'm easy,
> Ted was born with joy to make
> Cotchelin run crazy.

SONG CXXXVII.

JAACK RATLIN WAS THE ABLEST SEAMAN.

Jack Ratlin was the ableſt ſeaman, None like him could hand, reef, and ſteer: No dang'rous toil but he'd encounter, With ſkill and in contempt of fear. In fight a lion: the battle end-ed, Meek as the bleating lamb he'd prove: Thus Jack had manners, courage, merit, Yet did he figh, and all for love.

'The fong, the jeft, the flowing liquor,
    For none of thefe had Jack regard:
He, while his mefsmates were carouſing,
    High fitting on the pendant yard,
Would think upon his fair one's beauties,
    Swore never from fuch charms to rove;
That truly he'd adore them living,
    And dying figh—to end his love.

The fame exprefs the crew commanded
    Once more to view their native land,
Amongft the reft, brought Jack fome tidings,
    Wou'd it had been his love's fair hand!
Oh fate! her death defac'd the letter;
    Inftant his pulfe forgot to move;
With quiv'ring lips, and eyes uplifted,
    He heav'd a figh—and dy'd for love.

SONG CXXXVIII.

Tune—" *Jack Ratlin was the ablest Seaman.*"

Behold the man that is unlucky,
    Not thro' neglect, by fate worn poor;
Tho' gen'rous, kind when he was wealthy,
    His friends to him are friends no more!
He finds in each the same like fellow,
    By trying those he had relieved;
Tho' men shake hands, drink health's, get mellow,
    Yet men by men are thus deceiv'd.

Where can he find a fellow creature
    To comfort him in his distress?
His old acquaintance proves a stranger,
    That us'd his friendship to profess.
Altho' a tear drop from his feeling,
    His selfish heart cannot be mov'd;
Then what avails his goodly preaching,
    Since gen'rous deeds cannot be prov'd.

But so it is in life among us,
    And give mankind their justly due,
'Tis hard to find one truly gen'rous,
    We all, at times, find this too true;
But if your friend he feels your sorrow,
    His tender heart's glad to relieve;
And when he thinks on you to-morrow,
    He's happy he had that to give.

SONG CXXXIX.

ADIEU, ADIEU, MY ONLY LIFE.

A-dieu, adieu, my on-ly life, My honour calls me from thee: Remember thou'rt a fol- dier's wife, Thofe tears but ill be-come thee. What tho' by du-ty I am call'd Where thun- dring cannons rattle; Where valour's felf might ftand appall'd, Where valour's felf might ftand appall'd; When on the wings of thy dear love,

To heaven a-bove thy fervent orisons are flown;

The tender pray'r thou put'st up there Shall call

a guardian angel down, Shall call a guardian

an-gel down, To watch me in the battle.

My safety thy fair truth shall be,
  As sword and buckler serving,
My life shall be more dear to me,
  Because of thy preserving.

Let peril come, let horror threat,
   Let thundr'ring cannons rattle,
I fearless seek the conflict's heat,
   Assur'd when on the wings of love,
      To heaven above, &c.

Enough,—with that benignant smile
   Some kindred god inspir'd thee,
Who saw thy bosom void of guile,
   Who wonder'd and admir'd thee:
I go, assur'd,—my life! adieu,
   Tho' thund'ring cannons rattle,
Tho' murd'ring carnage stalk in view,
   When on the wings of thy true love,
      To heaven above, &c.

SONG CXL.

MY NANNY, O.

While some for pleasure pawn their health,

'Twixt Lais and the Bagnio, I'll save my-

self, and without stealth, Bless and caress my

Anny, O. She bids more fair t'engage a

Jove, Than Leda did, or Danae, O: Were

I to paint the Queen of Love, None else should

fit but Nan--ny, O.

How joyfully my spirits rife,
   When dancing she moves finely—O,
I guefs what heav'n is by her eyes,
   Which sparkle so divinely—O.
Attend my vow, ye gods, while I
   Breathe in the blest Britannia,
None's happinefs I shall envy,
   As long's ye grant me Nanny—O.

   My bonny, bonny Nanny—O,
   My lovely charming Nanny—O;
   I care not tho' the whole world know
   How dearly I love Nanny—O.

SONG CXLI.

WALY, WALY.

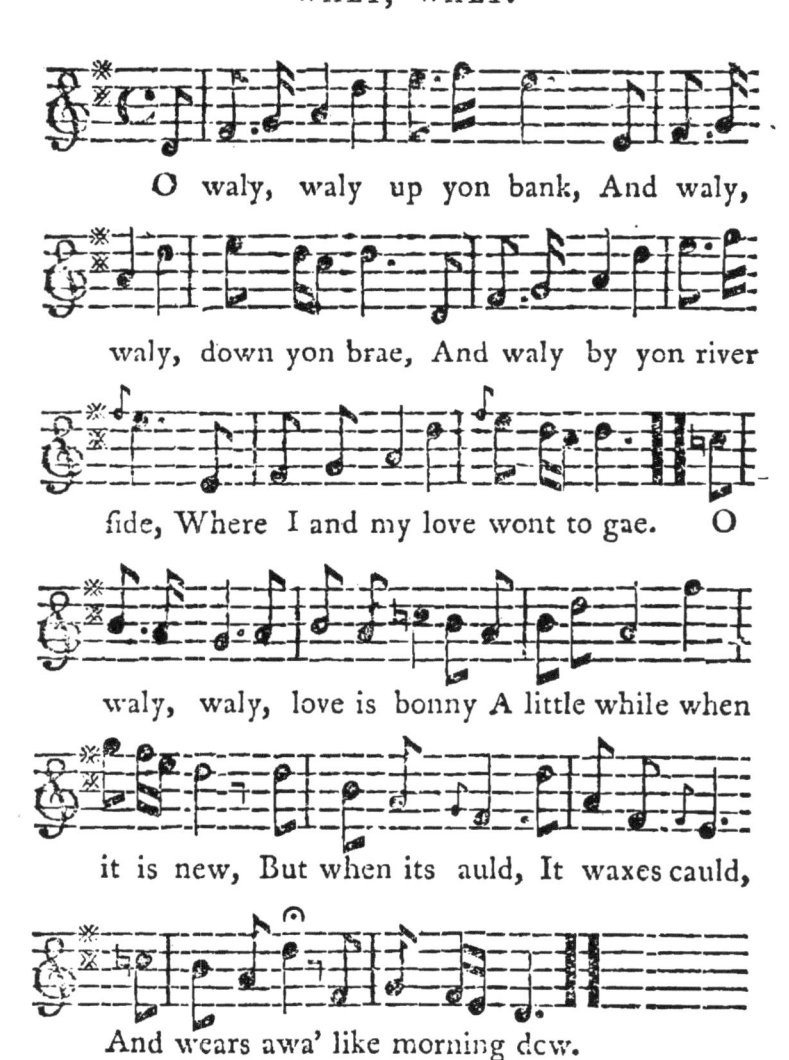

O waly, waly up yon bank, And waly, waly, down yon brae, And waly by yon river fide, Where I and my love wont to gae. O waly, waly, love is bonny A little while when it is new, But when its auld, It waxes cauld, And wears awa' like morning dew.

I lent my back unto an aik,
    I thought it was a trufty tree :
But firft it bow'd and then it brake,
    And fae did my faufe love to me.
When cockle-fhells turn filver bells,
    And muffels grow on ev'ry tree ;
When Froft and Snaw fhall warm us a',
    Then fhall my love prove true to me.

Now Arthur's feat fhall be my bed,
    The fheets fhall ne'er be fyl'd by me ;
St. Anton's well fhall be my drink,
    Since my true love's forfaken me.
O Mart'mas wind, when wilt thou blow,
    And fhake the green leaves off the tree ?
O gentle death, when wilt thou come,
    And take a life that wearies me ?

'Tis not the froft that freezes fell,
    Nor blawing fnaw's inclemency ;
'Tis not fic'cauld that makes me cry,
    But my love's heart grown cauld to me.
When we came in by Glafgow town,
    We were a comely fight to fee,
My love was cled in velvet black,
    And I myfell in cramafie.

But had I wift before I kift,
    That love had been fae ill to win ;

I'd lock'd my heart in cafe of gold,
   And pin'd it with a filver pin.
Oh! Oh! if my young babe were born,
   And fet upon the nurfe's knee,
And I myfel' were dead and gane,
   For maid again I'll never be!

SONG CXLII.

HERE AWA, THERE AWA.

Here a-wa, there awa, here awa, Willie,

Here awa, there awa, here awa hame. Lang

have I fought thee, dear have I bought thee,

Now I ha'e gotten my Willie again.

Through the lang muir I have followed my Willie,
Through the lang muir I have followed him hame :
Whatever betide us, nought shall divide us;
Love now rewards all my sorrow and pain.

Here awa, there awa, here awa Willie,
Here awa, there awa, here awa hame;
Come Love, believe me, nothing can grieve me,
Ilka thing pleases while Willy's at hame.

SONG CXLIII.

LOVE IS THE CAUSE OF MY MOURNING.

By a murmuring stream a fair shepherdess lay, Be so kind, O ye nymphs, I oft heard her say, Tell Strephon I die, if he pas-ses this way, And love is the cause of my mourn-ing.

False shepherds that tell me of beauty and charms, Deceive me, for Strephon's cold heart ne-ver warms: Yet bring me this Strephon, I'll die

in his arms, O Strephon! the cause of my

mourn-ing But first, said she, let me go, Down

to the shades below, Ere ye let Strephon know

That I have lov'd him so, Then on my pale

cheeks no blushes will shew That love is the cause

of my mourn--ing.

Her eyes were fcarce clos'd when Strephon came by,
He thought fhe'd been fleeping, and foftly drew nigh:
But finding her breathlefs, Oh heavens! did he cry,
   Ah Chloris! the caufe of my mourning!
Reftore me my Chloris, ye nymphs ufe your art.
They fighing reply'd, 'Twas yourfelf fhot the dart,
That wounded the tender young fhepherdefs' heart,
   And kill'd the poor Chloris with mourning.
      Ah! then is Chloris dead!
      Wounded by me! he faid,
      I'll follow thee, chafte maid,
      Down to the filent fhade!
Then on her cold fnowy breaft leaning his head,
   Expir'd the poor Strephon with mourning!

SONG CXLIV.

AT POLWART ON THE GREEN.

At Polwart on the green, If you'll meet me the morn, Where laffes do convene, To dance about the thorn. A kindly welcome'you shall meet Frae her wha likes to view A lover and a lad compleat, The lad and lo-ver you.

Let dorty dames say na,
As lang as e'er they please,
Seem caulder than the snaw,
While inwardly they bleeze:
But I will frankly shaw my mind,
   And yield my heart to thee;
Be ever to the captive kind,
   That langs nae to be free.

At Polwart on the green,
Amang the new mawn hay,
With sangs and dancing keen,
We'll pass the heartsome day:
At night, if beds be o'er thrang laid,
   And thou be twin'd of thine,
Thou shalt be welcome, my dear lad,
   To take a part of mine.

SONG CXLV.

BLEST AS THE IMMORTAL GODS IS HE.

Bleſt as th' immortal gods is he, The youth

who fondly ſits by thee, and hears and ſees thee

all the while, So ſoft-ly ſpeak, and ſweetly

ſmile. 'Twas this bereav'd my ſoul of reſt,

And rais'd ſuch tumults in my breaſt; For while

I gaz'd, in tranſport toſt, My breath was gone

My voice was loft.

My bofom glow'd, the fubtile flame
Ran quick thro' all my vital frame:
O'er my dim eyes a darknefs hung,
My ears with hollow murmurs rung.

In dewy damps my limbs were chill'd,
My blood with gentle horrors thrill'd,
My feeble pulfe forgot to play,
I fainted, funk, and dy'd away!

SONG CXLVI.

JOHN HAY'S BONNY LASSIE.

By smooth winding Tay a swain was reclining,

Aft cry'd he, Oh hey! maun I still live pining

Mysell thus a---way, And darena dis-cover

To my bon-ny lass that I am her lover.

Nae mair it will hide, the flame waxes stronger,

If she's not my bride, my days are nae longer

Then I'll tak' a heart, and try at a venture, May be, e'er we part, my vows may content her.

She's fresh as the spring, and sweet as Aurora,
When birds mount and sing, bidding day a good morrow:
The sward on the mead, ennamell'd with daisies,
Look wither'd and dead, when twin'd of her graces.

But if she appear where verdure invite her,
The fountains run clear, and the flowers smell the sweeter.
'Tis heaven to be by, when her wit is a flowing,
Her smiles and bright eye set my spirits a-glowing.

The mair that I gaze, the deeper I'm wounded;
Struck dumb with amaze, my mind is confounded;
I'm all in a fire, dear maid, to carefs ye,
For a' my defire is Hay's bonny Lassie.

SONG CXLVII.

THE BONNIEST LASS IN A' THE WARLD.

Look where my dear Hamilia smiles, Hami-

li-a heav'nly charmer; See how with all their

arts and wiles the loves and gra - ces arm

her A blush dwells glowing on her cheek,

Fair seat of youthful pleasure, There love in

smil - ing language speaks, There spreads the

ro - - fy trea - fure.

 O faireft maid, I own thy power,
  I gaze, I figh, I languifh,
 Yet ever, ever will adore,
  And triumph in my anguifh.
 But eafe, O charmer, eafe my care,
  And let my torments move thee;
 As thou art faireft of the fair,
  So I the deareft love thee.

SONG CXLVIII.

COPORAL CASEY.

When I was at home, I was merry and frisky, My dad kept a pig, and my mother fold whisky: My uncle was rich, but would never be ea-fy, 'Till I was inlifted by Corporal Cafey. Oh! rub a dub, row de dow, Corporal Cafey, rub a dub, row de dow, Corporal Cafey

My dear little Sheelah, I thought would run crazy, Oh! When I trudg'd away with tough Corporal Cafey.

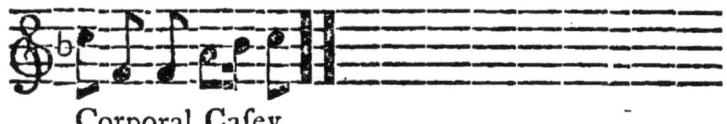

I march'd from Kilkenny, and as I was thinking
On Sheelah, my heart in my bofom was finking;
But foon I was forc'd to look frefh as a daifey,
For fear of a drubbing from Corporal Cafey.
Och! rub a dub, row de dow, Corporal Cafey!
The devil go with him! I ne'er could be lazy,
He ftuck in my fkirts fo, ould Corporal Cafey.

We went into battle, I took the blows fairly
That fell on my pate, but they bother'd me rarely;
And who fhould the firft be that dropt?—why, an't
    pleafe ye,
It was my good friend, honeft Corporal Cafey:
Och! rub a dub, row de dow, Corporal Cafey.
Thinks I you are quiet, and I fhall be eafy,
So eight years I fought without Corporal Cafey.

SONG CXLIX.

MY DEARY IF THOU DIE.

Love never more shall give me pain, My fancy's fixt on thee; Nor ever maid my heart shall gain, My Peg-gy if thou die. Thy beauty doth such pleasure give, Thy love so true to me, Without thee I can ne-ver live, My dea-ry if thou die.

If fate shall tear thee from my breast,
    How shall I lonely stray?
In dreary dreams the night I'll waste,
    In sighs the silent day.
I ne'er can so much virtue find,
    Nor such perfection see:
Then I'll renounce all woman-kind,
    My Peggy, after thee.

No new-blown beauty fires my heart
    With Cupid's raving rage,
But thine which can such sweets impart,
    Must all the world engage.
'Twas this, that like the morning sun,
    Gave joy and life to me;
And when it's destin'd day is done,
    With Peggy let me die.

Ye powers that smile on virtuous love,
    And in such pleasure share;
You who it's faithful flames approve,
    With pity view the fair.
Restore my Peggy's wonted charms,
    Those charms so dear to me;
Oh! never rob them from these arms:
    I'm lost, if Peggy die.

SONG CL.

SAW YE NAE MY PEGGY.

Saw ye nae my Peg-gy, Saw ye nae my Peg-gy, Saw ye nae my Peggy coming o'er the lee? Sure a finer creature Ne'er was form'd by nature, So compleat each feature, So divine is she. O how Peg-gy charms me, ev'ry look still warms me, Ev'ry thought

alarms me, Left she love not me. Peg-gy

doth dif-co-ver, Nought but charms all ever,

Na--ture bids me love her, that's a law

to me.

Who would leave a lover,
To become a rover?
No, I'll ne'er give over,
 Till I happy be.
For since love inspires me,
As her beauty fires me,
And her absence tires me,
 Nought can please but she.
When I hope to gain her,
Fate seems to detain her,
Could I but obtain her,
 Happy would I be!
I'll ly down before her,
Bless, sigh, and adore her,
With faint looks implore her,
 Till she pity me,

SONG CLI.

MY AIN KIND DEARY, O.

Will ye gang o'er the lee-rigg, My ain kind deary O, And cuddle there sae kindly, Wi' me, my kind deary O. At thornie dike, and birken tree, We'll daff, and ne'er be weary, O: They'll scug ill een frae you and me. Mine ain kind deary O.

Nae herds wi' kent, or colly there,
    Shall ever come to fear ye, O;
But lav'rocks, whistling in the air,
    Shall woo, like me, their deary, O!

While others herd their lambs and ewes,
    And toil for warld's gear, my jo,
Upon the lee my pleasure grows,
    Wi' you, my kind deary, O.

SONG CLII.
ALLAN WATER.

What numbers shall the muse repeat ! What verse be found to praise my Annie ? On her ten thousand gra-ces wait, Each swain admires and owns she's bon-ny. Since first she trode the hap-py plain, She set each youthful heart on fire: Each nymph does to her swain complain That Annie kindles new de - - fire.

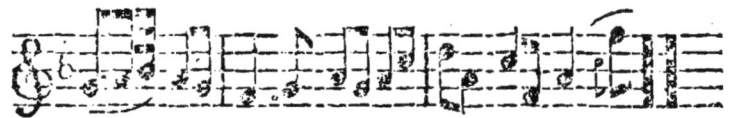

This lovely darling, dearest care,
   This new delight, this charming Annie,
Like summer's dawn she's fresh and fair,
   When Flora's fragrant breezes fan ye.
All day the am'rous youths convene,
   Joyous they sport and play before her;
All night, when she no more is seen,
   In blissful dreams they still adore her.

Among the crowd Amyntor came,
   He look'd, he lov'd, he bow'd to Annie;
His rising sighs express his flame,
   His words were few, his wishes many.
With smiles the lovely maid reply'd,
   Kind shepherd, why should I deceive you?
Alas! your love must be deny'd,
   This destin'd breast can ne'er relieve you.

Young Damon came with Cupid's art,
   His wiles, his smiles, his charms beguiling,
He stole away my virgin heart—
   Cease, poor Amyntor! cease bewailing:
Some brighter beauty you may find;
   On yonder plain the nymphs are many;
Then chuse some heart that's unconfin'd,
   And leave to Damon his own Annie.

SONG CLIII.

GREEN GROW THE RASHES.

There's nought but care on ev'ry han' In ev'ry hour that passes, O: What signifies the life o' man, An' twere not for the lasses, O? Green grow the rashes, O; Green grow the rashes, O, The sweetest hours that e'er I spend Are spent a-mong the lasses, O.

The warl'y race may riches chace,
    And riches ſtill may flee them O ;
An' tho' at laſt they catch them faſt,
    Their hearts can ne'er enjoy them, O.
        Green grow, &c.

But gi'e me a canny hour at e'en,
    My arms about my dearie, O :
An' warl'y cares, an' warl'y men
    May a' gae tapſailteerie, O !
        Green grow, &c.

For you ſae douſe ye ſneer at this,
    Ye're nought but ſenſeleſs aſſes, O :
The wiſeſt man the warl' ſaw,
    He dearly lov'd the laſſes, O.
        Green grow, &c.

Auld Nature ſwears the lovely dears
    Her nobleſt work ſhe claſſes, O :
Her prentice han' ſhe try'd on man,
    And then ſhe made the laſſes, O.
        Green grow, &c.

SONG CLIV.

THERE'S MY THUMB I'LL NE'ER BEGUILE THEE.

Bet--ty ear-ly gone a may-ing, Met her lover Willie ſtraying, Drift or chance no matter whither, This we know he reaſon'd with-her: Mark, dear maid, the turtles coo-ing, Fondly bil-ling, kind--ly woo-ing See, how ev'-ry buſh diſ-covers happy pairs of feather'd lo - vers.

See, the op'ning blush of roses
All their secret charms discloses;
Sweet's the time, ah! short's the measure;
O their fleeting hasty pleasure!
Quickly we must snatch the favour,
Of their soft and fragrant flavour;
They bloom to-day, and fade to-morrow,
Droop their heads, and die in sorrow.

Time, my Bess, will leave no traces
Of those beauties, of those graces;
Youth and love forbid our staying;
Love and youth abhor delaying;
Dearest maid, nay, do not fly me;
Let your pride no more deny me;
Never doubt your faithful Willie:
There's my thumb I'll ne'er beguile thee.

SONG CLV.

HER ABSENCE WILL NOT ALTER ME.

Though diftant far from Jef-fy's charms, I ftretch in vain my longing arms, Though part-ed by the depths of fea, Her abfence fhall not al-ter me. Tho' beauteous nymphs I fee a-round, A Chloris, Flo-ra, might be found, Or Phyl-lis with her rov-ing eye: Her abfence shall not al - - ter me.

A fairer face, a sweeter smile,
Inconstant lovers may beguile,
But to my lass I'll constant be,
Nor shall her absence alter me.
Though laid on India's burning coast,
Or on the wide Atlantic tost,
My mind from love no pow'r could free,
Nor could her absence alter me.

See how the flow'r that courts the sun
Pursues him till his race is run!
See how the needle seeks the Pole,
Nor distance can its pow'r controul!
Shall lifeless flow'rs the sun pursue,
The needle to the Pole prove true;
Like them shall I not faithful be,
Or shall her absence alter me?

Ask, who has seen the turtle dove
Unfaithful to its marrow prove?
Or who the bleating ewe has seen
Desert her lambkin on the green?
Shall beasts and birds, inferior far
To us, display their love and care?

Shall they in union sweet agree,
And shall her absence alter me?

For conqu'ring love is strong as death,
Like vehement flames his pow'rful breath,
Thro' floods unmov'd his course he keeps,
Ev'n thro' the sea's devouring deeps:
His vehement flames my bosom burn,
Unchang'd they blaze till thy return;
My faithful Jessy then shall see,
Her absence has not alter'd me.

SONG CLVI.

LOCH-EROCH SIDE.

As I came by Loch Eroch side, The lofty hills surveying, The water clear, the heather blooms Their fragrance sweet conveying.

I

met unsought, my lovely maid, I found her like May-morning; With graces sweet and charms so rare, her person all adorning. Person all adorning.

How kind her looks, how blest was I,
  When in my arms I press'd her!
And she her wishes scarce conceal'd,
  As fondly I caress'd her.
She said, if that your heart be true,
  If constantly you'll love me,
I heed not cares, nor fortune's frowns,
  Nor ought but death shall move me.

But faithful, loving, true, and kind,
  Forever you shall find me,
And of our meeting here so sweet,
  Loch Eroch side will mind me.
Enraptur'd then, " My lovely lass!
  I cry'd, no more we'll tarry,
We'll leave the fair Loch Eroch side,
  For lovers soon should marry."

SONG CLVII.

YOUNG PEGGY.

Tune—*Loch Eroch Side.*

Young Peggy blooms our bonnieſt laſs,
    Her bluſh is like the morning,
The roſy dawn, the ſpringing graſs,
    With early gems adorning:
Her eyes outſhine the radiant beams
    That gild the paſſing ſhower,
And glitter o'er the chryſtal ſtreams,
    And chear each freſh'ning flower.

Her lips more than the cherries bright,
    A richer dye has grac'd them,
They charm th' admiring gazer's ſight
    And ſweetly tempt to taſte them:
Her ſmile is as the ev'ning mild,
    When feath'red pairs are courting,
And little lambkins wanton wild,
    In playful bands diſporting.

Were fortune lovely Peggy's foe,
    Such ſweetneſs would relent her,
As blooming ſpring unbends the brow
    Of ſurly, ſavage winter.
Detraction's eye no aim can gain
    Her winning pow'rs to leſſen:

And fretful envy grins in vain,
  The poifon'd tooth to faften.

Ye pow'rs of Honour, Love, and Truth,
  From ev'ry ill defend her;
Infpire the highly favour'd youth
  The diftinies intend her;
Still fan the fweet connubial flame
  Refponfive in each bofom;
And blefs the dear parental name
  With many a filial bloffom.

SONG CLVIII.

THE LASS OF LIVINGTON.

Pain'd with her flighting Jamie's love, Bell dropt a tear, Bell dropt a tear; The gods descended from a-bove, Well pleas'd to hear, well pleas'd to hear: They heard the praises of the youth, From her own tongue, From her own tongue, Who now converted was to truth, And thus she sung, and thus she sung.

Bless'd days when our ingenuous sex,
   More frank and kind—more frank and kind,
Did not their lov'd adorers vex,
   But spoke their mind—but spoke their mind:
Repenting now, she promis'd fair,
   Wou'd he return—wou'd he return,
She ne'er again wou'd give him care,
   Or cause him mourn—or cause him mourn.

Why lov'd I the deserving swain,
   Yet still thought shame—yet still thought shame,
When he my yielding heart did gain,
   To own my flame—to own my flame?
Why took I pleasure to torment,
   And seem too coy—and seem too coy.
Which makes me now, alas! lament
   My slighted joy—my slighted joy?

Ye Fair, while beauty's in its spring,
   Own your desire—own your desire,
While love's young pow'r with his soft wing
   Fans up the fire—fans up the fire!
O do not with a silly pride,
   Or low design—or low design,
Refuse to be a happy bride,
   But answer plain—but answer plain.

Thus the fair mourner wail'd her crime
With flowing eyes,—with flowing eyes,
Glad Jamie heard her all the time,
With sweet surprize,—with sweet surprise.
Some god had led him to the grove,
His mind unchang'd,—his mind unchang'd,
Flew to her arms, and cry'd, my love,
I am reveng'd,—I am reveng'd.

SONG CLIX.

LOGIE OF BUCHAN.

O Logie of Buchan, O Logie the Laird,
They ha'e ta'en awa' Jamie that delv'd in the yard! Who play'd on the pipe, wi the viol sae sma', They ha'e taen awa Jamie the flow'r o'

them a'. He said, think na lang, lassie, tho' I

gang a-wa; He said, Think na lang lassie, tho'

I gang awa': For the simmer is coming, cauld

winters awa, And I'll come and see thee, in

spite o' them a'

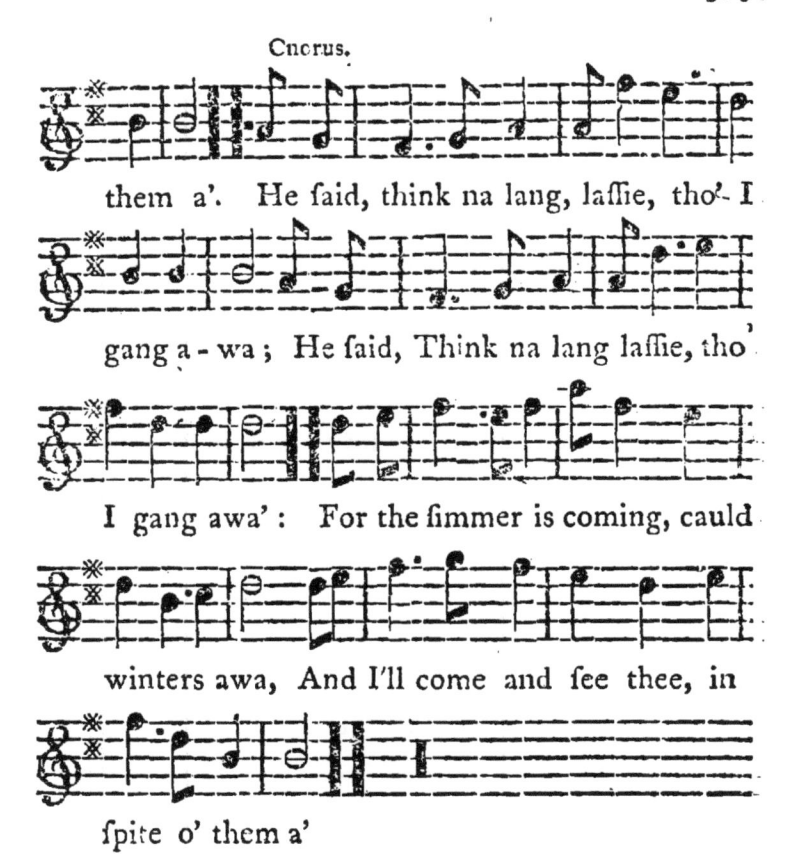

Sandy has ousen, has gear, and has kye;
A house, and a hadden, and siller forby:
But I'd tak' mine ain lad, wi' his staff in his hand,
Before I'd ha'e him, wi' his houses and land.
    He said, think na lang lassie, &c.

My daddy looks sulky, my minny looks sour;
They frown upon Jamie, because he is poor:

Tho' I lo'e them as well as a daughter fhould do,
They are nae half fae dear to me, Jamie, as you.
  He faid, think na lang laffie, &c.

I fit on my creepie, and fpin at my wheel,
And think on the laddie that lo'ed me fo weel;
He had but ae faxpence, he brak it in twa,
And he gied me the ha'f o't when he gaed awa.

  Then hafte ye back, Jamie, and bide na awa.
  Then hafte ye back, Jamie, and bide na awa.
  Simmer is coming, cauld winter's awa,
  And ye'll come and fee me, in fpite o' them a'.

SONG CLX.

THE NUN'S COMPLAINT.

In this fad and filent gloom loft Lou-i-fa pines unknown, Shrouded in a living tomb,

Doom'd to pine a---lone. Midst the

si-lent shades of woe, Tears of fond re-

gret shall flow, Tears of fond re-gret---

---et shall --------flow. Tell, soft

lute, in plaintive tone, Sad Lou--i--sa's hap-

less moan, Midst the si-lent shades of woe,

Still the tears must flow.

Ye dark clouds, who sail along,
Hide me in your shade profound;
Whisp'ring breezes bear my song,
   To the woods around.
Should some pensive lover's feet,
Wander near this sad retreat,
   Tell, soft lute, &c.

Tell her, love's celestial tale
Yields no bliss, no joy inspires,
Cold religion's icy veil
   Darkens all his fires.
No soft ray adorns the gloom,
Round the hapless vestal's tomb
   Tell, soft lute, &c.

Fancy's flame within my breast,
Faintly glows with vital heat;
Tender passions sink to rest—
   Soft my pulses beat!
Soon these languid eyes shall close,
Death's cold dart shall seal my woes!
   Tell, soft lute, &c.

SONG CLXI.

THE KNITTING GIRL.

Hark, Phillis, hark, thro' yon-der grove,

Responsive Nature sings; Love seeks the deep

embowerd alcove, and lends swift Fancy wings.

Phillis heard, but Phillis sat, silent knitting,

silent knitting at her cottage gate: Phillis heard

but sat silent knitting at her cottage gate.

Enthron'd, he's seated in thine eye,
  Where he, tho' blind, can see
Himself reflected in each sigh,
  He bids me breathe for thee.
    Phillis heard, &c.

Lo! tow'rds the bow'r he beckons now,
  O rise, and come away!
From ill to ward thee is his vow,
  To guard, and not betray.
    Phillis heard, but Phillis sat
    No longer knitting at her cottage gate.

SONG CLXII.

ALLOA HOUSE.

The spring time returns, and cloaths the green plains, And Alloa shines more chearful and gay; The lark tunes his throat, and the

neighbouring swains sing merrily round me where-
e-ver I stray; But Sandy no more returns to my view! No spring time me chears,
no music can charm, He's gone, and I fear
me for ever adieu! Adieu, ev'ry pleasure
this bosom can warm!

O Alloa house! how much art thou chang'd!
How silent, how dull to me is each grove!
Alone I here wander where once we both rang'd,
Alas! where to please me my Sandy once strove!

Here Sandy I heard the tales that you told;
Here liftened too fond, whenever you fung;
Am I grown lefs fair, then, that you are turn'd cold?
Or foolifh, believ'd a falfe, flattering tongue;

So fpoke the fair maid; when forrow's keen pain,
And fhame, her laft fault'ring accents fuppreft:
For fate at that moment brought back her dear fwain,
Who heard, and, with rapture, his Nelly addreft:
My Nelly! my fair, I come; O my Love,
No power fhall thee tear again from my arm,
And, Nelly! no more thy fond fhepherd reprove,
Who knows thy fair worth, and adores all thy charms.

She heard; and new joy fhot thro' her foft frame,
And will you, my love! be true? fhe reply'd.
And live I to meet my fond fhepherd the fame?
Or dream I that Sandy will make me his bride?
O Nelly! I live to find thee ftill kind;
Still true to thy fwain, and lovely as true;
Then adieu! to all forrow: what foul is fo blind
As not to live happy for ever with you?

AT EDINBURGH:
PRINTED BY GRANT & MOIR,
Anno 1793.